IN SIX DAYS GOD CREATED

Refuting the Framework and Figurative Views of the Days of Creation

PAULIN BÉDARD

In Six Days God Created
Refuting the Framework and Figurative Views of the Days of Creation
by Paulin Bédard

Printed in the United States of America

ISBN 9781625092991

www.xulonpress.com

TABLE OF CONTENTS

Acknowledgments ix

Introduction 11
The necessity to address the framework interpretation 11
The origin of the framework interpretation 12
Summary of the framework interpretation 14

I. The literal interpretation is satisfactory 17
1. The days 21
The cardinal number of day one 21
The definite article of the sixth and seventh days 23
No evening and no morning on the seventh day 24
2. The fourth day 28
The alleged problem 28
The light 30
The day and the night 32
The lights in the expanse created on the fourth day 34
Genesis 1:2 and the "problems" solved on the fourth day 39
Theological implications 42
3. Genesis 2:4 and the meaning of "day" 45
4. Genesis 2:5 49

We must be cautious with new theories 49
The alleged meaning and scope of Genesis 2:5 50
Some difficulties with this interpretation of Genesis 2:5 51
Other possible interpretations of Genesis 2:5 55
The alleged principle drawn from Genesis 2:5 pushed to the absurd 59
Theological implications 64
5. Genesis 2:19 66

II. The framework interpretation is problematic 69
1. "Literal" 71
2. The structure in two triads 72
A parallel between the first day and the fourth day? 74
A parallel between the second day and the fifth day? 76
A parallel between the third day and the sixth day? 80
Three "problems" structuring the six days? 83
Other possible literary structures 88
3. False dilemmas 89
A refined literary composition vs the literal meaning 89
Thematic structure vs strictly chronological meaning 94
Meaning and purpose vs facts and history 98
4. The unending seventh day 103
5. "Background" 109
6. The analogy of faith 115
The book of Genesis—its genre, outline and content 115
Day, evening, and morning in the Pentateuch 117
Exodus 20:8–11 118
The light in other Scripture passages 122
7. Other problems 125
The age of the earth when Adam was created 125

The source of our knowledge of God's way of creating 127

III. The framework interpretation is dangerous 129

1. Doubts on what God really said 131
2. Rejection of the historicity of some events 132
3. More corrosive effects of this approach 136
4. The centrality of the present reality 141
5. The deceptiveness of the Word of God 148
6. A "pre-scientific" solid heavenly dome 153
7. A false view of God's accommodation 158
8. God's inability to communicate accurately 162
9. "Heavenly time" and complete skepticism 164
10. The lack of clarity of Scripture 169
11. A source of division in the Church 172
12. The pervasive influence of modern secular science 173
13. The origin of our seven-day week 186

Conclusion 189

Endnotes 195

Bibliography 233

Index of Authors 249

ACKNOWLEDGMENTS

I am deeply thankful to the Lord who gave me the strength and the joy to write this book, and who guided me toward several individuals who were of tremendous help and encouragement throughout the entire project.

I wish to thank the members of my congregation, the Église chrétienne réformée de Beauce (affiliated with the Église réformée du Québec), and especially the members of my consistory. They kept encouraging me to take time every week to study the Word of God, read theological books, and work on different types of material, which proved to be useful for the edification of the Church and the deepening of the knowledge of God's Word.

I would like to express my deep gratitude to Mrs. Francine VanWoudenberg Sikkema for all the time and energy she spent reading through my manuscript several times and correcting the countless mistakes of the first draft. I am very grateful for her professional proof-reading, without which the publication of this book would have been impossible. I fear new mistakes might have appeared—for which she is obviously not responsible—in the paragraphs I added at different places in the manuscript after her last careful reading. . .

I also would like to warmly thank the persons who willingly read over my manuscript, and who made many corrections and suggested several modifications, which greatly improved both the content and the form of the text. I am indebted to Dr. Wes Bredenhof, Dr. John Byl, Dr. Anco Farenhorst, Rev. Peter Feenstra, Dr. Margaret Helder, Rev. Peter Holtvlüwer, Dr. Jannes Smith, and Dr. Cornelis Van Dam for those improvements. In many ways, they have encouraged me to carry on with this project and bring it to completion. I am especially indebted to my friend Peter Feenstra who first suggested that I translate into English the research article I wrote on the subject, which was first published in French.[1] Several important additions have been made to this article after its translation, so that the present book is now much more extended.

I want to express my heartfelt gratitude to my beloved wife Claire for her constant love, her patience with me, and her unfailing support, as well as for the corrections she has made to the text.

Finally, I would like to express my deep gratitude to the Canadian Reformed Church of Owen Sound, in Ontario, and to other churches and individuals of their federation involved with them. I am deeply touched by the extremely generous support and constant encouragement, during the past thirteen years, that they have shown to me and to the church that I serve. Their love for the Word, their faithful prayers, their brotherly love, and their precious advice have been a source of inspiration for my work and an encouragement to continue serving the Lord and His Church. I know that their desire is that the Good News of Jesus Christ be preached to the French-speaking people in the province of Quebec, and that the Church of our Lord be gathered and edified by the faithful preaching and teaching of His Word. As a mark of gratitude to the Lord for their faithful support, my desire, in return, is that this book be beneficial to their federation and to many other churches in the English-speaking world.

It is my hope and prayer that this work may bring glory to God and contribute to the edification of His Church.

INTRODUCTION

The necessity to address the framework interpretation

During the past two centuries, the truth that God has clearly revealed to us about the origin of the world has been greatly undermined, if not completely rejected, by numerous scientists and theologians. Many Christians, pastors, and church leaders nowadays are being influenced by modern secular scientific opinion with its assumption that the earth is billions of years old and its aggressive promotion of the evolutionary model.

In this context, many new ways of interpreting the creation account of Genesis 1 have been proposed to the Christian community. This includes the framework hypothesis and other figurative interpretations, which are now being propounded by a number of theologians and pastors. The framework hypothesis does not come from professed unbelievers but from people who profess to believe in the authority of the Bible and who wish to remain faithful to Scripture.[2] They assert that their interpretation is based strictly on exegetical grounds. We shall see, however, that the framework hypothesis is problematic in many ways.

The growing popularity of the framework hypothesis in several Evangelical and Reformed circles is astonishing, considering the fact that it has already been criticized by many on exegetical and theological grounds.[3] It is surprising to see how widespread it is in many seminaries and churches, which are now being contaminated by its pervasive influence.[4]

Unfortunately, many do not seem to see either the insidious character of such a position or its far-reaching consequences. Some may say that the issue of the specific meaning of the creation days is not that important, or that the framework interpretation may be an acceptable or a neutral position after all. I, however, have become convinced that this subject is very important and that the framework interpretation is a very dangerous error in churches today. My concern is that this interpretation attacks the Word of God in a subtle and insidious way,[5] even though many of those who uphold this interpretation do not seem to be conscious of its problems and have a sincere desire to be faithful to the text of Holy Scripture. Nonetheless, the end result of this interpretation is that it reduces the authority of the Bible, introduces novel hermeneutics, and undermines the biblical doctrine of creation.

In the past, many churches have given way to the appeal of establishing a synthesis between the atheistic theory of evolution and the biblical doctrine of creation, and then have rapidly sunk into unbelief. Considering the devastating effects of the attacks against the historicity of the creation account, we must take very seriously the way we understand the first page of the Bible.[6] It is thus imperative to address the framework and figurative views of the creation account in the light of God's Word.

The origin of the framework interpretation

Proponents and opponents of the framework interpretation usually consider A. Noordtzij, who taught at the University of Utrecht, as the father of the framework view of the creation days. It is the opinion of Lee Irons and Meredith G. Kline that:

> Dutch theologian Arie Noordtzij pioneered this approach to the creation week in 1924. The substance of his work has been made available in English by N. H. Ridderbos in his book *Is There a Conflict Between Genesis 1 and Natural Science?* published in the United States in 1957. Ridderbos presents a popular treatment of the framework interpretation and depends heavily on the work of Noordtzij, whom he cites extensively.[7]

Marc Kay has a different opinion and considers Johan Gottfried von Herder as the father of the theory:

> The German philosopher Johann Gottfried von Herder (1744–1803), remonstrating against the harsh rationalism of the Enlightenment, stated that the "history of the creation [account] is entirely a sensuous representation arranged by days' work and numbers; in seven pictures of the separate portions of the created universe; and placed with reference to their parallel or corresponding relations."[8]

Henri Blocher agrees and says that it was "Herder [who] recognized the powerful symmetry between the two triads of days."[9]

In 1958, Kline published an article promoting the framework view based on a new interpretation of Genesis 2:5.[10] In 1996, he published a second article presenting a restatement of his arguments with a new line of reasoning based on his more recent "two-register cosmology."[11] Kline taught at Westminster Seminary both in Philadelphia and in California, as well as at Gordon-Conwell. He is seen as the most influential scholar to have promoted the framework interpretation, although not all the framework proponents adhere to his two-register cosmological concept.

Summary of the framework interpretation

There are different versions of the framework hypothesis, but the most widely known seems to be that propounded by Kline. Irons, together with Kline, formulated the following definition of the framework interpretation:

> It is that interpretation of Genesis 1:1–2:3 which regards the seven-day scheme as a figurative framework. While the six days of creation are presented as normal solar days, according to the framework interpretation the total picture of God's completing His creative work in a week of days is not to be taken literally. Instead it functions as a literary structure in which the creative works of God have been narrated in a topical order. The days are like picture frames. Within each day-frame, Moses gives us a snapshot of divine creative activity. Although the creative fiat-fulfillments (e.g., "Then God said, Let there be light [fiat]; and there was light [fulfillment]") refer to actual historical events that actually occurred, they are narrated in a nonsequential order within the literary structure or framework of a seven-day week. Thus, there are two essential elements of the framework interpretation: the nonliteral element and the nonsequential element.[12]

Most of the proponents of this interpretation firmly assert the historicity of the events reported in Genesis 1–2. The framework proponents, however, must face this important question: How does the negation of the timescale and sequence of events affect the nature and the historicity of these events? Are they not related to each other? Besides, it is noteworthy that the two essential criteria defining the theory are presented in a negative manner: *nonliteral* days and *nonsequential* order. According to this view, it seems easier to find out what the days are not rather than what they really are.

To be sure, as a literary device, the figurative or metaphorical week has a positive function (like picture frames) in the creative account. The topical arrangement is intended to teach us truths about God, man, the world, and the relationship between them. But what are the theological teachings of Genesis 1 that we are really missing when we accept the creation days as real literal sequential days? The framework proponents assert that their interpretation brings several theological concepts to light, such as a pattern for work, a Sabbath theology, a covenant theology, a polemic against idolatry, a doxology to the glory of God the Creator, etc. But all these teachings advocated by the framework proponents are included in the literal interpretation.

Irons and Kline state that the advocates of the framework interpretation base their view:

> On the ground of several prominent features of the text. . .: (1) the two-triad structure of the account; (2) the temporal recapitulation of Day 1 at Day 4; (3) the evidence from Genesis 2:5–6; (4) the eternal nature of the seventh day; and (5) in Kline's case, the two-register cosmology that constitutes both the literary and theological marrow of the creation account.[13]

These arguments, it is supposed, demonstrate the impossibility of a literal sequential understanding of the days of creation. Other proponents of the figurative interpretation, sympathetic to the framework view without fully endorsing it, reject the so-called "traditional interpretation" on more or less similar grounds. For example, W. Robert Godfrey expresses some hesitations and mild criticism regarding the framework interpretation but maintains that "the days of creation are figurative descriptions of the actions of God." He enumerates five problems that exist for the traditional interpretation, borrowing ideas from the framework view.[14]

This essay is an attempt to discuss and criticize the aforementioned arguments.[15] We will see that the arguments are not based on solid grounds and that they raise more problems than they solve. The main points proposed in favour of the framework interpretation will be scrutinized, first by showing that the objections to the literal interpretation are not justified, second by indicating important problems related to the framework hypothesis, and finally by considering more closely the real dangers related to this theory.

I

THE LITERAL INTERPRETATION IS SATISFACTORY

Before we examine each argument in favour of the framework interpretation and some of its different figurative variants, we must underline the fact that, in order to justify its existence, the framework interpretation must frequently emphasize that the literal interpretation is not satisfactory. If there were no difficulties in the literal interpretation, why should we look for solutions? It seems important for the framework proponents to find problems to solve, otherwise who would be prepared to listen to their very complex solutions? R. C. Sproul, who recently abandoned the framework interpretation and now holds to a literal six-day creation, says, "One must do a great deal of hermeneutical gymnastics to escape the plain meaning of Genesis 1 to 2."[16] But frankly, are the alleged problems of the literal position so real? Are they as serious as the framework proponents maintain?

1

The Days

The cardinal number of day one

The framework interpretation affirms that the six days of creation are to be taken neither literally nor sequentially but should be understood as figurative. In support of this theory, the framework proponents discern *literary refinements* in the account of creation. This leads them to conclude that the inspired author did not intend to present a chronological sequence of creative acts that took place in the space of six literal days, but rather a picture frame of creative acts presented in a thematic order.

Apparently, many literary clues cause difficulties to the literal reading of the first chapter of Genesis. For example, in Genesis 1:5 the first day is called "day one" in Hebrew, instead of "the first day." R. S. Ward noted that:

> The first day is more correctly translated "day one"; the next four days lack a definite article, contrary to many translations, and thus should read, "a second day," etc., whereas days six and seven have the definite article. Such features are not found in a series of ordinary days.[17]

However, we do not see why the presence of a cardinal number for "day one" would cause problems with the chronological and sequential understanding of the days of creation. The use of the cardinal number "one" followed by the ordinal numbers "second," "third," etc. appears rather frequently in the Mosaic books.

For example, in the context of the creation account of the garden of Eden it says, "the name of the river *one*. . ., the name of the *second* river. . ., of the *third* river. . ., of the *fourth* river. . ." (Gen. 2:11–14); Lamech's wives, "the *one* Adah, the *second* Zillah" (Gen. 4:19); "In the year 601, in the month *one*. . . the waters were dried up from the earth. . . In the *second* month. . . the earth was dried" (Gen. 8:13–14).[18] We find other examples in Exodus 1:15; 25:12, 32; 26:4–5, 10, 26–27; 28:10, 17; 29:15, 19, 39–41; 36:11–12, 17, 31–32; 37:3, 18; 39:10–13; etc. In not one of these cases in the Pentateuch does the cardinal number "one" followed by an ordinal number ("second," etc.) indicate a figurative meaning. The rivers of the garden are not figurative, neither are Lamech's wives, nor the first two months of the year 601 of Noah, etc. Why, then, would the cardinal number "one" in Genesis 1 be a clue indicating that the days are to be taken figuratively?

An author has the freedom to enumerate a series of days of ordinary length in more than one way. Besides, "when an ordinal number is used with *yom* not one example of non-sequence can be fond [sic]."[19] When we read Genesis 1, it is not difficult even for a child to understand the order indicated in a chronological way: day one, second day, third day, fourth day, fifth day, the sixth day, the seventh day. This is especially true when we consider that between each day the summary statement is given by "an evening and a morning," words that are never used metaphorically in Scripture but are used consistently in reference to literal days.[20]

The definite article of the sixth and seventh days

The fact that the days two to five have no definite article is another example of a literary clue apparently favouring the framework interpretation. According to Ward quoted in a preceding paragraph, this detail would seem to add weight to the idea that the days of creation should be taken figuratively.[21]

But again, one wonders where the difficulty is. The presence of two definite articles on the sixth and seventh days and the absence of definite articles with the five preceding days is no reason to question the literal character and the sequential historicity of the days. The framework proponents understand that the text really speaks about seven days and about a complete week. Of course, they consider these days and this week to be metaphorical, that is to say, we should take them figuratively and not literally. But when they read Genesis 1, the cardinal number of day one and the definite articles of day six and day seven do not prevent them, like anybody else, from counting an entire week, seven days with evenings and mornings.

W. R. Godfrey, a proponent of the figurative interpretation who shows affinity to the framework interpretation but questions some of Kline's detailed exegesis, notices this literary detail. He says that it indicates one of the seven different uses of the word "day" that he detects in Genesis 1:1–2:4. However, Godfrey does not prove nor even suggest that the definite article on the sixth and seventh days gives a different meaning to the word "day." He simply says that "this shift from 'day five' to 'the day six' and 'the day seven' is another way in which Moses highlighted the importance of those days in the text."[22]

After having raised the "difficulty" of the cardinal number and of the definite articles, the framework interpretation does not give a better solution to this "problem." In order to harmoniously correspond to the parallelism of the two triads (days one to three supposedly being parallel to days four to six), one would expect that the first three days be without a definite article and that the last three days be with a definite article, or that the first three days be designated by cardinal numbers (one, two, three) and that the last three by ordinal numbers (fourth, fifth, sixth), or something like that. If the author of Genesis is apparently so fond of literary devices, why did he not match these stylistic details to the overall pattern? The framework or the literary device in two triads is definitely not the solution.

The answer sometimes given is that the definite article before the sixth and the seventh days are there for reasons of emphasis. But if there really is an emphasis in the days, this emphasis may actually reveal a *historical progression* in the temporal sequence of the creative work. Why should the reasons of emphasis and the chronology be opposed to each other? With the sixth and the seventh days, we come to the historical and sequential end of the week of creation, and, at the same time, we also come to the climax of the creative work of God. Thus, the details in Hebrew show that the sixth day is the culminating day of creation, and that the seventh day was a special day because God had finished His work of creation.[23]

Besides, the framework proponents acknowledge that the creative work ends with the creation of the man and the woman (*the* sixth day), and then climaxes in the communion with their Creator in the joy of His rest (*the* seventh day). The presence of definite articles with the sixth and seventh days serves this purpose perfectly: to highlight *both* a historical accomplishment *and* a theological climax, or more precisely to strengthen the theological meaning by the historical and chronological data. In conclusion, the definite articles of the sixth and seventh days harmonize very well with a temporal sequence of normal days.

No evening and no morning on the seventh day[24]

Many have observed that the seventh day has no evening. Would this literary clue not give us permission to believe that the seventh day does not have a normal duration? Many insist that the seventh day has a perpetual or an eternal nature.[25] We would then be permitted to interpret the other days differently than literally. "The final exegetical observation that ultimately clinches the case [for the framework interpretation] is the unending nature of the seventh day."[26]

We first observe that on the seventh day the text not only omits mentioning the evening but also the morning. Therefore, the question is this: Why is there no evening *and no morning*? This detail is important. Each of the first six days ends with the refrain: "And there was evening and there was morning." Why is this refrain absent on the seventh day? It is for the simple reason that this refrain is present the rest of the week not only to give rhythm to the *chronology* of the days; it also gives rhythm to the *progression* of the work of God in time during the week of creation. "And there was evening and there was morning. . ."

This expression fulfils the double function of *closing* the day that is just finished and of *opening* the scene to the next day. The new morning that begins places us in the expectation of a new word of God. After day one, what will the Lord do now on the second day? After the second day, what will He do on the third day? And after the sixth day, what will He do on the seventh day? "And there was evening and there was morning, the sixth day." What word will God pronounce now? This time no creative word is spoken; instead, there is a word of accomplishment – a word that decrees an end to His achieved creative work, and at the same time a word that calls the man and the woman to rejoice with God in this accomplished work. He rested from His work, blessed the seventh day, and sanctified it. It would then be surprising to have the account of the seventh day end with: "And there was evening and there was morning." There is nothing to expect on the next day regarding the creative work of God. All His creative work is accomplished; the seventh day marks the conclusion of this work.

The absence of the expression "And there was evening and there was morning" does not mean that the seventh day did not actually end with an evening followed by a morning the next day. This is an argument from silence—one which contradicts Exodus 20:11. Genesis 2:1–3 does not say that the seventh day did not have an evening; nor does it say that it was not followed by a morning. Adam and Eve had enjoyed blessed communion with their Creator during a complete day of worship and relaxation on the seventh day. They went to sleep peacefully the evening of the seventh day before undertaking their work the next day, when the sun rose on the very good creation of the Lord. The inspired text uses all the possible means available to let us know that the creative work of God is really *finished* and that Adam and Eve may enjoy the blessedness of God's communion during their first full day on earth. R. V. McCabe's additional comments are useful in this regard:

> The evening-morning conclusion is one part of a fivefold structure that Moses employed in shaping the literary fabric for each of the days of the creation week. None of the other parts of this fivefold arrangement are mentioned on the seventh day. Moses used this fivefold pattern to represent, in a brief yet accurate manner, God's creation of the heavens, the earth, and all things therein in the space of six, sequentially numbered, literal days. By excluding the fivefold pattern, Moses' theological emphasis was to demonstrate in literary form that Day 7 was a day of cessation from divine creative activity. This is to say the omission of the evening-morning conclusion is related to the omission of the other four parts of this fivefold pattern. Since the other four parts are not needed in that God's creative activity is finished, this concluding formula was not needed either. This overall structuring device was not utilized for the apparent reason that God is no longer creating after Day 6. Because Day 7 is a historic literal day, it is numbered like the previous six days.[27]

> Finally, the seventh day must be a literal day because God blessed and sanctified it. If the seventh day is unending, this means that not only did God bless and sanctify it, but he also, on the same unending day, cursed the earth with the Fall of Genesis 3. From a theological perspective, this is questionable. "We must assume," as John Whitcomb has astutely observed, "that the seventh day was a literal day because Adam and Eve lived through it before God drove them out of the Garden. Surely, he would not have cursed the earth during the seventh day which he blessed and sanctified."[28]

This is also Gentry's opinion:

> If true, it would imply no fall and curse (Gen. 3), for then God would be continually hallowing and blessing that "ongoing day." In fact, God does not bless His eternal rest, but a particular day.[29]

In conclusion, the absence of any mention of evening and morning on the seventh day is in complete harmony with the literal interpretation.

2

The Fourth Day[30]

The alleged problem

The framework proponents make a great fuss about the alleged "problem" of the creation of the sun on the fourth day.[31] They wonder how the first three days can be days of normal length when the "signs to mark seasons and days and years" were not created yet. It is not difficult to address this question, and the Genesis account itself gives the answer.

God, on the very first day, created the light, separated the light from the darkness, and established the alternation of day and night. We do not know the details, but there was obviously a source of "alternative" light, or of "direct" light combined with the rotation of the earth, or another kind of physical phenomenon enabling such an alternation of day and night during the first three days before it was handed over to the sun and the moon on the fourth day. From that moment on, beginning on the fourth day, these luminaries would be signs to mark seasons and days and years.

But this explanation is not satisfactory for the framework proponents. They consider the fourth day to be a *recapitulation* of day one. In other words, it is "a description of the same event from a different angle, with added information."[32] The reason given is that the same language is used for both days. On the first day, God "separated the light from the darkness" (1:4), and on the fourth day, God created the lights "to separate the light from the darkness" (1:18). The framework proponents conclude from this that the two days do not describe different activities, separated in time by three days, but contemporaneous activities, *the same event* seen from two different perspectives. M. Futato says:

> Either God's work on Day 4 is redundant, reaccomplishing the same thing he had already accomplished on Day 1, or the accounts of God's work on Days 1 and 4 are two different perspectives on the same creative work. . . The repetition of language binds the work of Days 1 and 4 together into a single activity.[33]

Moreover, how can the light, the day, and the night exist without the sun, the moon, and the stars? It is contrary to our present experience, and it is different from the normal providential means God provided for the alternation of day and night, the way it is seen today. According to Futato, our knowledge of the real world signals an overlay of day one and day four. He asserts that there must be such an overlay, since "lexical repetitions abound between Day 1 and Day 4, and light without luminaries is not part of the real world in which the original audience lived."[34]

Thus, according to the framework proponents, the first three "days" must be ordinary solar days, governed and illuminated by the sun. The "nights" must be ordinary nights, governed and illuminated by the moon and the stars. Consequently, the six days of creation could not represent a chronological order but should be taken in a figurative manner. The whole week is taken as a metaphor, but this is precisely what the book of Genesis *does not say*; as a matter of fact, it says exactly the contrary.

The light

Let us look at the first day. The light of the first day is created by an authoritative word: "And God said, 'Let there be light'" (1:3). According to Genesis 1, the light is the result of the creative Word alone. The text does not say that God created a *source* that gives out light or that the light depends on the sun and the stars; the text says that He created the *light* itself. Once the light is created, there are various possibilities as to where the light originates. Before God spoke, of course, nothing existed. When He spoke, it all came into being. The light, which was created on the very first day, may or may not have emanated from a source. The Bible does not disclose this information one way or the other.[35]

Besides, it cannot be proven that the presence of the light requires the existence of sources of light that we observe today. Are the sun and the moon necessary in order to have light? What about lightning?[36] "Even in Big Bang cosmology light is assumed to appear long before the formation of the Sun and stars."[37] God first created the phenomenon of electromagnetic energy, then He created the sun and the stars, which produce (or reflect, in the case of the moon) such waves. Similarly the air for the propagation of the sound waves was created before musical instruments.

The text confirms that this light is established: "And there was light" (1:3). Here is an additional indication that the work mentioned is completed. God speaks authoritatively, and here is the result. Then, the Lord evaluates it positively: "And God saw that the light was good" (1:4). The text expresses forcefully that the light is *complete in itself.* The work of God pleased Him. The light was created the way He had wanted it, to serve the purpose for which He created it.

The judgment "good" is repeated seven times in Genesis 1, and each time it represents fullness, the creation of something complete in itself (the light, the dry ground and the seas, the vegetation, the lights, the creatures of the sea and the birds, the man, and finally the whole creation). Why would the light be an exception? Why would it be the only thing not complete in itself? If the light would not have been complete without the sun, the "good" evaluation should at least have been omitted, as on the second day, for example. The only work that is not declared "good" is that which was created on the second day, probably because it was not yet complete. The water under the heavens needed to be gathered into "seas" on the third day so that both the "seas" and the "dry land" could receive their inhabitants. Godfrey says:

> Many interpreters have observed that God does not declare his acts on the second day as good. Why is that? The first reason is that God had not completed his work on the waters. By withholding his word of evaluation God points to the fact that the work on the waters is not completed until the third day. Only then does he call it good.[38]

Godfrey, however, is not consistent. He does not apply this insight to the first day. He does not see the light as a created reality that is complete in itself, but he follows the framework proponents on this point and believes that "the lights that fill the sky. . . always were the source of light. In other words, day one and day four describe the same creative act of God from different perspectives."[39]

One more detail: The light is the only "good" created reality that is specifically mentioned in the evaluation. "And God saw that the light was good" (1:4). For the other created realities, the text says in a more general way, "And God saw that it was good." It is only at the end of the creation week, on the sixth day, that the created reality is again mentioned after the verb "saw." Verse 31 reads as follows: "And God saw everything that he had made, and behold, it was very good." This verse echoes verse 4. The first work of creation is declared good; then the whole creation, when completed, is declared very good. These two verses punctuate the temporal *beginning* and the temporal *end* of the created works.

The light is obviously sequentially created at the beginning. Everything points to the fact that it is a work of God complete in itself that does not need the sun for its existence.[40]

The day and the night

L. Irons and M. G. Kline say this:

> The text makes clear that when God created daylight on the first day, He created the physical reality with which Moses' audience was familiar; namely, a normal day divided into alternating periods of light and darkness (Gen. 1:5). Doesn't the plain meaning of Genesis 1:3–5 contradict Duncan and Hall's hypothetical nonsolar light source? And shouldn't this fact suggest that the fourth day is not to be taken sequentially and so is separated from the first day?[41]

It is true that God created a day divided into alternating periods of light and darkness. Nevertheless, the text does not say that these alternating periods of light and darkness were produced by the sun, or that this first day already presented a "physical reality with which Moses' audience was familiar." To read this into Genesis 1:3–5 is at least as hypothetical as the possibility of a nonsolar light source.

After having created the light, God separated the light from the darkness. Then He defined the words that would be used afterwards. It is interesting to see that the Bible gives a definition of the word "day" right at the first occurrence of the word in the Bible: "God called the *light Day* and he called the *darkness Night*" (1:5). The day is defined in relation to the light, as opposed to the night, which is defined in relation to the darkness. This must be taken into consideration in the rest of the narrative. Immediately after the definition is given, it is said, "And there was evening and there was morning: *day* one." The day is naturally understood first as a period of brightness as opposed to the night. Then it is naturally understood as the whole day including the evening and the morning. From the first day to the second day, the complete cycle of a normal day occurred.

It is noteworthy, as well, that the day and the night are not defined in relation to the sun and to the moon, but strictly in relation to the light and the darkness. The Bible does not say, "God called the sun 'day' and he called the moon and the stars 'night.'" The sun is not necessary for determining a day; all that is required is the light alternating with the darkness, even though it is not our daily experience today. Actually, the alternation of the light and darkness for determining a day *is* our daily experience today, except that there has been a progression in the works of God since the first day of creation, so that this present alternation of light and darkness is now governed by the lights created on the fourth day.

As for the past conditions, let us not forget that we know very little about the unique and extraordinary period of creation.[42] It is very risky to try to impose the prevailing conditions that we observe today, especially because God's creative works were not finished yet and because the conditions prevailing during the extraordinary week of creation necessarily changed dramatically from one day to another.[43]

There were actually alternating periods of darkness and light during the first three days, but Genesis 1 does not say anywhere that those first three days and those first three nights were governed by the sun and the moon.[44] For this reason, it is not correct to say, as Kline affirms in his definition of his interpretation, that "the six days of creation are presented as normal solar days."[45] The first three days are not normal solar days at all. The creation of the sun is mentioned only on the fourth day. According to Genesis 1:3–5, the day is simply defined by the *alternation* of the darkness of the evening and the brightness of the morning, and not by the rotation of the earth illuminated by the sun.

The lights in the expanse created on the fourth day

It is true that the separation of the light from the darkness on the fourth day has similarities with that which happened on the first day. What does that prove? Simply that there is a *continuity* between what God already accomplished on the first day and what the lights would accomplish from then on—a historical continuity, and not a recapitulation. For on the first day, God Himself separated the light from the darkness, whereas on the fourth day, God gives this function to the lights (sun, moon and stars). Is that not a noteworthy difference?

There are two different activities as opposed to just one. The one is *directly* accomplished by God; the other is *indirectly* accomplished by the lights. On the first day, God created the light, and He established the alternation of day and night, whereas on the fourth day, the only creative word pronounced is the one producing the lights. No creative word is pronounced here concerning the day or the light. These two days are very different, and it is certainly significant. God created lights not to create or define the day and the night but only to *separate* them. He continued to keep them separate, as they were separated during the first three days, but from now on by a different means. The means by which light was now separated from darkness was by the activity of the sun, moon, and stars.

On the fourth day, the creative word presupposes the pre-existence of the earth. "And let them be lights. . . to give light upon the earth" (1:15). It also presupposes the pre-existence of the expanse. "Let there be lights in the expanse of the heavens" (1:14). It finally also presupposes the existence of the light prior to the fourth day, as well as the pre-existence of the day and of the night. "Let there be lights. . . to separate the day from the night" (1:14). When the creative word is executed, the text also says that "God made the two great lights. . . to rule the day. . . and to rule the night" (1:16). The text does not say that which is "ruled" has been created or produced by the "ruler." The day and the night are simply created realities *distinct* from the lights and *ruled* by them. All this shows us that the cycle of day and night really existed before the creation of the sun.

It is interesting to note that the light, which was created on the first day, was established ("and there was light," 1:3) and was immediately declared "good" ("And God saw that the light was good," 1:4). On the other hand, on the same day, when God separated the light from the darkness to form "an evening and a morning," the text does not say that the situation was "established" or that God declared it "good." The text simply says, "And there was evening and there was morning: day one" (1:5). On the one hand, the separation of the light from the darkness was *sufficient* to establish the alternation of day and night, and on the other hand, this separation was unfinished, *incomplete* in comparison with God's whole plan. The more definitive and providential mechanism of separation of the light from the darkness (the sun, the moon, and the stars) is not created before the fourth day. When God said "Let there be lights in the expanse of the heavens to separate the day from the night" (1:14), the Creator resumed the work He had left unfinished on the first day.

The framework proponents ask why God should have made a replacement mechanism.[46] They cannot conceive of such a possible change, because they think that God should have abolished an order established for a short period of three days to immediately establish another order right on the fourth day. The work of separation of the first day, however, is precisely not "established" yet. Therefore, God does not abolish the work of the first day. He does not recapitulate, either; He *adds* and *completes*. The work progresses as time goes by. On the fourth day His action to "separate" the light from the darkness comes for the first time to a decisive stage, a stage where it is now "established": "And it was so" (1:15).

God put the lights in the expanse "to rule over the day and over the night, and to separate the light from the darkness" (1:18). It is immediately followed by a global evaluation of His work of the fourth day: "And God saw that it was good" (1:18). This positive evaluation applies as much to the creation of the lights as to the separation of the light from the darkness. This separation is now "good," completed, achieved, because the astronomical mechanism has just been created. From now on it will be the "normal" means established by God for the alternation of day and night.

The framework proponents still object that on the first day God called the light "day" and the darkness "night" and that He consequently established their essential nature and their significance. If their nature has changed, then their names should have changed on the fourth day, too.[47] The plain answer is that the nature of the day and of the night has not actually changed. The day is still a period of light, and the night is still a period of darkness. The sun and the moon do not determine the nature of the day and of the night; they *govern* them. Consequently there is no need to change their names. We just need to take their names seriously, *literally*, according to the definition given by God Himself on the very first day!

This is why on the fourth, fifth, and sixth days there is still "an evening and a morning: the *n*th day" without the slightest hint of modification to the rhythm when passing from the third day to the fourth day. The function of the light is *handed over* to the lights, but the alternation of day and night continues exactly as it did during the first three days. The sun and the moon are created to be *perfectly fit* for the cycle of day and night, which already exists, and not the reverse. Therefore, the first three days are all the same length as the following days, ordinary-length days, and not years or ages. Genesis 1 is crystal clear!

M. G. Kline says:

> [The sun, moon, and stars] are to give light on the earth and to rule by bounding light/day and darkness/night, as well as by demarcating the passage of years and suc-

> cession of seasons. These effects which are said to result from the production and positioning of the lights on day four are the same effects that are already attributed to the creative activity of day one (Gen. 1:3–5).[48]

This is plainly false! The effects resulting from the production and positioning of the lights on day four are *not* all the same as those attributed to the creative activity of day one. Godfrey repeats the same error made by Kline when he says, "The closeness of the relationship is underscored by the identity of words used on the two days and especially by the reiteration of the function of the lights (Gen. 1:14–18)."[49] Day one and day four do not just reveal a reiteration, they reveal a *progression*.

To be sure, light and lights both have the same effect on the succession of the days. They both separate the day from the night, and light from darkness. The lights, however, do much more. The sun and the moon also receive the function "to rule over the day and over the night" (1:18), a function that was not attributed to the light on the first day. Moreover, to the succession of the days, the lights add the succession of seasons and years: "And let them be for signs and for seasons, and for days and years" (1:14). We find nothing of that sort on the first day. During the first three days, the alternation of light and darkness permitted only the succession of days and nights. After the sun, the moon, and the stars are created, the revolution of the earth around the sun begins, producing the succession of seasons and years. The moon begins to revolve around the earth, allowing the succession of lunar months. We see no such thing on the first day. The light alone could not assume such a function.

From day one to day four, there is a tremendous progression in the cosmological and astronomical order. We can marvel at God's wisdom in preparing a wonderful and adequate habitat for man, where man will learn to number his days, seasons, and years. At the end of the fourth day, however, one temporal rhythm is still missing, a rhythm not based on any physical or astronomical phenomenon. The rhythm of the seven-day week will have to be established in a different way, at the end of the creation week.

Godfrey sees a first problem for the traditional interpretation: "Only three of the seven days of Genesis 1 are described as normal days, namely, with a sun to shine and an evening and morning."[50] This is no problem at all when one is open to the fact that some of the creation days are not "normal days" with a sun to shine or with the ending "evening and morning." Godfrey is guilty of circular reasoning. He first posits that a "normal day" must be with a sun to shine and must mention "evening and morning." Then he concludes that some of the days of Genesis 1 are not "normal," thus apparently causing difficulty to the traditional interpretation. His definition of "normality" is based on our present observation of the sun and moon ruling our days and nights, not on the text of Scripture.

Considering the progressive creative work of God, there is no problem at all to see the first three days of creation as "special days" (not governed by the sun), of normal length with normal succession of light and darkness, punctuated by normal evenings and mornings. Neither is there any problem to see the seventh day as a "special day" of rest of normal length ruled by the sun (without the mention of "evening and morning" for the reason explained in a previous paragraph).

The second problem that Godfrey sees for the traditional interpretation ("the traditional view does not explain the identities between day one and day four presented in the text"[51]) is simply a false problem. As it has been shown, there is no complete identity between these two days in the text. It is the figurative view that does not explain the tremendous progression observed from day one to day four.

The framework proponents see the parallel between the first day and the fourth day in the context of a so-called two-triad parallelism. According to this structure, the "filling" elements in the second triad (fourth, fifth, and sixth days) should actually fill habitats that already exist. These habitats must have been previously created in the first triad (first, second, and third days), before their inhabitants are placed in them. For example, the fish were created to fill the seas, whereas the animals of the earth and the man were created to fill the earth. When the fish, the animals of the earth, and the man are created, the seas and the earth must already exist. Why should it be different for the first and fourth days? The fourth day should add something to what has already been created previously. The second and the fifth days cannot represent two aspects of the same creative act any more than the third and sixth days. Mark Ross, when discussing the so-called "form and fullness" topical arrangement, recognizes this fact:

> The point is not that no sequence can be found in the passage. It stands to reason that before the great sea-creatures can swarm in the sea there must first be seas; and before plants can grow on the dry ground there must first be dry ground; and before birds can fly in the sky there must first be a sky.[52]

Yes, indeed! Why, then, insist that in the presumed parallelism of the two triads the fourth day would be a recapitulation of the first day? This approach seems inconsistent. When God created man to fill the earth and subdue the animals, these animals already existed. The creation of man, the "steward" or "governor," did not bring the animals into existence. Likewise, the creation of the sun and of the moon as "governors" did not bring into existence the light, the day, and the night.[53] This confirms again the pre-existence of the light over the sun.

Genesis 1:2 and the "problems" solved on the fourth day

Godfrey sees a somewhat different literary pattern in Genesis 1 based on the "problems" mentioned in Genesis 1:2 ("The earth was without form and void, and darkness was over the face of the deep. . .") but concludes, like the other framework proponents, that days one and four describe the same creative act.

> The idea of a different source for light on the first three days is certainly possible since our God can do whatever pleases him. . . The traditional interpretation, however, does not give adequate attention to the way in which the days of creation are addressing the problems of Genesis 1:2. The creation of the lights on day four is addressing not the problem of darkness but the problem of the emptiness of the sky. The text seems to suggest that day four is not about the creation of a new and different source for the light created on day one but rather is now pointing us to the lights that fill the sky and that always were the source of light. In other words, day one and day four describe the same creative act of God from different perspectives and as solutions to different problems posed in Genesis 1:2.[54]

When Godfrey says that "the text seems to suggest that day four is not about the creation of a new and different source for the light. . .," and that the lights "always were the source of light," he does not prove anything from the text but simply affirms what he would like to see in the text.

Regarding the way in which the days of creation are addressing the problems of Genesis 1:2, the "traditional interpretation" gives a very satisfying answer. God had two solutions to at least two different problems, applied at two different moments. On the first day, God solved the problem of darkness by the creation of the light. Three days later, He solved the problem of emptiness of the sky by the creation of the lights. Also, it is not excluded that one creative act may solve more than one "problem." The lights not only solve (partly) the problem of emptiness of the sky, they also continue to solve the problem of darkness. They are "to give light upon the earth" (1:15). Moreover, their creation also gives form and order to the cosmos and to its astronomical laws. They are to function as signs for seasons, days, and years. On the fourth day, one single creative act solves three problems in the expanse of the heavens—forming, filling, and giving light. When we look for literary devices in Scripture, we should be careful not to reduce God's manifold wisdom to a simple literary pattern.

The theory of the recapitulation entails another insurmountable problem. On the fourth day, God said, "Let there be lights *in the expanse*. . ." (1:14), which, once again, implies the pre-existence of this expanse. We know that the expanse was created on the second day (1:7). If the fourth day is just a recapitulation of the first day, if the two describe the same event, this means that the reality created on the second day (the expanse) appeared chronologically *earlier* to the reality created on the first and fourth days.

The framework proponents say that this is not a problem since the days are not sequential. The problem is, however, that it is grammatically impossible. E. J. Young has shown that verse 3 is grammatically linked to verse 2. He suggests that the three circumstantial clauses of verse 2 must be construed with the verb "said" of verse three. "We may then paraphrase, 'At the time when God said, Let there be light, a three-fold condition was in existence, namely, *etc.*'"[55] In other words, when God pronounced the words "Let there be light," He did so *in the context* of the earth being still formless, empty, and dark (the water created initially). It is not possible that the expanse (a beginning of formation) was created before the light. Otherwise, the grammar of the text does not mean anything. Therefore, the light must be the first work of God in the context of the initial creation of the earth as formless, empty, and dark.

L. Irons and M. G. Kline say, "The temporal recapitulation of Day 1 on Day 4 justifies taking the whole week of seven days as a figurative framework that provides a literary and theological structure for the narrative of the divine work of creation."[56] But if there is no such temporal recapitulation, as has been shown, the supposed justification for taking the whole week of seven days as a figurative framework has disappeared. On the other hand, if the creative events of days one and four are clearly presented in a chronological and sequential order, showing a tremendous historical progression, as we have established, this clearly reinforces the literal reading of the whole week of seven days.

Theological implications

Time has its origin in God's creative acts and is very important for God's plan, right from the beginning. If Genesis 1:3–5 does describe a real historical event, it must be understood that the alternation of day and night is not the effect of the lights but of *the direct or special action of God.* In the beginning, God created the light Himself, He Himself separated the light from the darkness, and then He started the cycle of day and night. This does not rule out other sources of light used during those first three days. God does not specify the source of light. It may be independent of a light source or it may be associated with the structures already created at that time. Originally, however, the time and the rhythm of time were not produced by the sun, moon, and stars, and were not ruled by normal providential means as we see them today. Originally, time and the rhythm of time were *miraculous acts of creation*. Exactly like the light, the expanse, the vegetation, and the birds were miraculous acts of creation.

It is significant that the history of the week of creation begins with the *creation* of time and of its rhythm and ends by the *sanctification* of time on the seventh day: "So God blessed the seventh day and made it holy" (2:3). Nowhere does Genesis 1 say that the earth, the seas, the fish, the birds, etc., were made holy. The text says that time, the seventh day, was made holy by God. This sanctification of the seventh day does not punctuate the cycle of day and night (already established on the first day), nor the cycle of seasons and years (established on the fourth day). It punctuates the cycle of the *week* now established by God Himself on the seventh day. Therefore, the created time is especially important in the eyes of God, and right from the beginning!

This should make us very cautious of accepting a figurative interpretation of time; indeed, this should even make us resist such an idea. If the creation of the oceans and the continents must be seen as real historical events, the creation of time must also be seen as a real historical event, including the rhythm God has given to time during the creation week. Space and time are closely connected in God's plan. Time in Genesis 1 is not a metaphor, it is a creation of God serving God's eternal purposes.

It is also significant that the light was created apart from the sun, the moon, and the stars. Some people have thought that this was a scientific mistake, but that is not the case anymore today.[57] The order of God's creation shows that the light comes from God. He created it. The light does not first come from the sun. The light is a gift of God, not a gift of the sun! It is marvellously *good news* for our naturalistic age, which believes that the sun by itself made life possible on earth. Some people are even frightened by the thought that one day solar energy will be exhausted. No, it is not the sun that must be worshipped, since the sun is just a part of the creation, but it is the Creator alone, the Giver of light, who must be worshipped!

E. J. Young has this word of wisdom:

> Light is the foundation of all that follows, but you may have wondered why the light is mentioned without the sun. There was a time when some men said that this was a scientific error, but men do not speak that way anymore. That the sun is not yet mentioned is deliberate. It is to show men that light comes from God, and that God is to be worshipped and not the sun. The ancient world was a sun-worshipping world. The Egyptian hieroglyphics speak of the god *Ra* who was the sun-god. . . In the ancient Near East, the concept of the sun is very prominent. There, where the sun is shining for the greater part of the day, sinful man would lift up his eyes, see the sun in the

> sky, and worship it as a god. But that we may understand that light, the necessary foundation for all life, is the gift of God and not of the sun, light is mentioned before the sun.[58]

John Calvin saw the importance of the creation of light before the sun. His commentary on Genesis 1:3 is wonderful:

> It was proper that the light, by means of which the world was to be adorned with such excellent beauty, should be first created; and this also was the commencement of the distinction (among the creatures). *It did not, however, happen from inconsideration or by accident, that the light preceded the sun and the moon.* To nothing are we more prone than to tie down the power of God to those instruments, the agency of which he employs. The sun and moon supply us with light: and, according to our notions, we so include this power to give light in them, that if they were taken away from the world, it would seem impossible for any light to remain. Therefore *the Lord, by the very order of the creation, bears witness that he holds in his hand the light, which he is able to impart to us without the sun and moon.*[59]

These words are beautiful and very encouraging! Calvin discerns a theological and a pastoral reason for the creation of the light before the lights, namely, that we may become attached to the Creator and not to the creation. Once again, his *Soli Deo Gloria* motif prevails; to God alone be the glory!

3

Genesis 2:4 And The Meaning Of "Day"

The fifth problem Godfrey sees for the traditional interpretation is that: "This view, insisting as it does that the meaning of 'day' in Genesis 1 is obviously a twenty-four-hour day, creates a contradiction between Genesis 1 and Genesis 2:4, where we are told that the whole creation occurred in a day."[60] Which day, he asks, is the literal day: the day of Genesis 1 or the day of Genesis 2:4? This question is easily answered by the fact that the noun "day" is used in two different grammatical contexts. In Genesis 1, "day" is a singular absolute, but in Genesis 2:4, it is a singular construct prefixed by *be*, thus *beyom*, often used as an idiomatic expression for "when."[61]

There is an exact parallel in Numbers 3:1: ". . .at the time (*beyom*) when the Lord spoke with Moses on Mount Sinai," when we know that Moses was on Mount Sinai forty days. There is an even more striking parallel in Numbers 7:10–84. In verses 10 and 84, at the beginning and at the end of the passage, *beyom* is used in relation to the whole twelve days of sacrifice at the consecration of the tabernacle. In between these, at verses 12, 18, 24, etc., we have *yom* used with a number to refer to each of the twelve literal days ("the first day," "on the second day," "on the third day," etc.). Nobody questions the historical reality and true chronological sequence of these days. In the same way, Genesis 1 carefully qualifies its creative days. Moreover, this is done after Genesis 1:5 has specifically defined its day as a true period of light, followed by the darkness called night, together forming a real literal day. On day four the sun is created to govern the day, so that from day four on the days are solar days. There is no ambiguity here.

Godfrey is not the first to see a discrepancy between the days of Genesis 1 and the alleged "day" of Genesis 2:4. Augustine espoused the possibility that God created everything simultaneously, partly because of his understanding of Genesis 2:4. In *The literal Meaning of Genesis* (5.3.6), he said that "the earlier narrative [Genesis 1] stated that all things were created and finished on six consecutive days, but now to one day everything is assigned, under the terms 'heaven' and 'earth.'"

It must be said, however, that Augustine did not know any Hebrew and only attained a modest knowledge of Greek by the end of his life, after he had written his four commentaries on the first chapters of Genesis. He was limited by his reliance upon the Old Latin version and argued from that version of Genesis 2:4, which reads: "This is the book of the creation of heaven and earth. When day was made, God made heaven and earth." Thus, Augustine partly based his allegorical interpretation on a translation of a translation (LXX), which erroneously translates *beyom* by "when day was made."[62] Additionally, Augustine quoted Sirach 18:1 to prove that God "created all things together." He mistakenly regarded this apocryphal book—which gives further support to the idea of an instant creation—as "Holy Scripture." Since Augustine is often improperly cited as a friend or even pioneer of the figurative view, it must also be pointed out that over the years he fluctuated between allegorical interpretations and literal views. Several other errors in the Old Latin version that he used did not help him clarify his understanding of Genesis 1.[63]

Godfrey himself repeatedly says that the days and the week of Genesis 1 are presented as "ordinary," "real," "actual" days and week. The different use of *beyom* in Genesis 2:4 does not preclude him from clearly understanding the normal use of *yom* in Genesis 1.

> All of our considerations of the Bible's teaching on days and time should lead us to the conclusion that the days and week of Genesis 1 are presented to us as a real week of twenty-four-hour days. These days and week, however, do not describe God's actions in themselves but present God's creative purpose in a way that is a model for us. The purpose and message of Genesis is that God created the world for humankind—a world in which man could be the image of God in his working and his resting.[64]

> We see that the days of Genesis 1 are ordinary twenty-four-hour days. But many pointers indicate that these ordinary days are for us as a model for our working, not as a time schedule that God followed. Those pointers include the character of God's rest on the seventh day, the identity of functions for the light and the lights uniting the first and fourth days, and the various ways in which the word *day* is used, particularly in Genesis 2:4. The days are actual for us but figurative for God. They are not a timetable of God's actions but are a model timetable for us to follow.[65]

Ultimately, the problem for Godfrey is not the meaning of the word "day" in Genesis 1, but its relevance to God's actions in themselves. What does it mean that "the days are actual for us but figurative for God"? This is the question asked by Jim Witteveen:

> But, speaking of "six actual historical days," this is where things get really muddy in Godfrey's book. Godfrey claims that the days of creation "are actual for us, but figurative for God" (p. 90). In response to a statement like

> this, I can only say that my mind is unable to wrap itself around such a concept. I'm not exactly sure how a day can be actual for God's creatures, but figurative for their Creator. Perhaps there's a metaphysical concept here that I'm not grasping, but if not, this statement is ultimately meaningless.[66]

Godfrey is correct when he says that the days of Genesis 1 are "all about the creation of the visible world, including the creation of day itself."[67] Nevertheless, since the days are as much a part of the creation of the world as the light, the sun or the animals, it would be absurd and meaningless to say that the light and the lights are actual for us but figurative for God, or that the dry land, the birds, the fish and the land animals are actual for us but figurative for God.

Yes, "the days were created for us, not for God, who always dwells above time in eternity."[68] This does not mean that the days are not real for God. The days were also created for God's glory. In the same way, we may say that the light, the expanse, the water, the dry land, the lights and all the animals were created for us, not for God, who always dwells above space and matter. Does that mean that they are not real for God? They were also created for God's glory. God lives in eternity, not with birds and fish. In His eternal glory and blessedness, He is not surrounded by the sun, the moon, and the stars, but He really created them all, including the light, the day, and the sun, which began to rule over the days on day four. But God also came into His creation, to speak, act, and walk "in time" with His creatures. Thus, the days of creation *are* primarily about God's creative acts in themselves and about the time it took God to create the world. Genesis 1 obviously reveals God's creative work *in space and time*, including the creation and ordering of space and time.

In conclusion, the idiomatic expression *beyom* in Genesis 2:4 does not change the clear and simple meaning of the word "day" in Genesis 1. The days of creation are as real and actual for God as they are for us.

4

Genesis 2:5

We must be cautious with new theories

We will now consider another argument the framework proponents have used. If God created all the plants of the field on a literal third day, then what is the meaning of Genesis 2:5? According to Kline and his followers, Genesis 2:5 teaches that plants did not come about until there was rain to water the earth, thus contradicting the order of the creation taught in Genesis 1. "When no bush of the field was yet in the land and no small plant of the field had yet sprung up – for the Lord God had not caused it to rain on the land, and there was no man to work the ground" (Gen. 2:5). Why should God be hesitant to make plants simply because there was no rain? Could not the plants have survived a couple of days without water? Especially when we consider that on the same third day that the vegetation was created on the earth, vast amounts of water were gathered to let the dry land appear. This dry land must still have been a little wet! In other words, the lack of rain should not have constituted a reason for not creating plants if God was using extraordinary providence during the creation week.

It is important to know that this argument from Genesis 2:5 was presented for the first time by Kline in an article published in 1958.[69] In his article, Kline proposes a new interpretation of Genesis 2:5. To our knowledge, this interpretation had never been proposed before 1958, and it paved the way for the present popularity of the framework interpretation. Henri Blocher says that this interpretation of Genesis 2:5 is "a new argument with a very striking power."[70] Mark D. Futato further develops Kline's arguments.[71] This new interpretation, if it is correct, would prove in a decisive way that Genesis 1 cannot be taken literally.

Of course, it is legitimate to try to find a better understanding of the Word of God, and it is always possible to correct past interpretations and to come to a new and more precise understanding of a verse of the Bible. However, we should be cautious when we are confronted with a new interpretation of a verse, especially when the claims of the new interpretation deeply affect the understanding of the *whole* account of creation. It seems that Kline and Futato want to prove a lot with this one verse. This new interpretation of Genesis 2:5—which some people call "eccentric"—not only seeks to clarify the meaning of *one verse*, but also has the effect of overturning the traditional interpretation of the *totality* of chapter 1 of Genesis.

The alleged meaning and scope of Genesis 2:5 [72]

Several framework proponents believe that, according to Genesis 2:5, God created the plants only after the normal conditions of life and growth of these plants were made effective, for example, after the Lord sent rain on the earth. Kline says:

> Verse 4 itself describes a time when the earth was without vegetation. And the significant fact is a very simple one. It is the fact that an explanation—a perfectly natural explanation—is given for the absence of vegetation at that time: "for the Lord God had not caused it to rain upon the earth." The Creator did not originate plant life on earth before he had prepared an environment in which he

> might preserve it without by-passing secondary means and without having recourse to extraordinary means such as marvelous methods of fertilization. The unargued presupposition of Genesis 2:5 is clearly that the divine providence was operating during the creation period through processes which any reader would recognize as normal in the natural world of his day.[73]

He applies this to the creation of plants on the third day. To be fair, Kline's interpretation does not deny God's supernatural creative acts or God's power to act supernaturally according to His sovereign will. What is denied is the use of *supernatural providential* acts during the period of creation. The creation of plants is miraculous, but the conservation of these plants was supposedly made possible only by "normal" providential means, such as those seen and known today. This means that the creation of plants could have happened only when the present normal conditions of survival for plants have been effectuated. This is not the case if we take Genesis 1 literally, because, for instance, the creation of the plants happened in only one day, on the third day, before the creation of the sun and before there was rain on the earth.

Moreover, the "normal" providence (i.e. a normal pattern of governing laws as we see today) for plant life is arbitrarily extended to *the whole* of the created works. After their creation, these works necessarily subsisted only by "normal" providential means, according to the theory.[74]

Some difficulties with this interpretation of Genesis 2:5

If Genesis 2:5 really teaches that God employed only ordinary providence to sustain His created works during the creation week, it is difficult to understand why, immediately afterward, the text says the Lord used an extraordinary or at least unusual means to water the whole surface of the ground: a mist or streams that came up from the earth (2:6). We do not see the Lord using such a means today.

Some framework proponents maintain that the rare and difficult word translated as "mist" or "streams" (*'ed*) necessarily designates a "rain cloud" produced by the ordinary providence of God.[75] Nothing in the text forces us to see it this way. What prevents the possibility that this "mist" was produced by extraordinary means? The text seems to point in this direction when it says that this one "mist" (singular) watered the whole surface of the ground. It is difficult to find normal meteorological conditions similar to this phenomenon on earth today. Moreover, according to the framework theory, this cloud must have watered the earth long enough to give the plants time to grow. To categorically maintain that it was necessarily a normal providential means goes too far. We know so little about it.

Furthermore, to be consistent, it should be said that God created the plants only after the creation of man. Genesis 2:5 notices two "deficiencies": no rain and no man to work the ground. Normally plants need rain and at least some plants need to be cultivated. Why, then, do the framework proponents still believe that man is temporally the last work to be created? Contrary to the opinion of most of the framework proponents, Godfrey says that "in Genesis 2:6 man seems to be created before the vegetation,"[76] creating for him a third problem for the traditional interpretation of Genesis 1, where the vegetation is created before man. Kline himself argues that:

> The implications of man's position as lord of creation, the scope of the cultural mandate, and other considerations require that the creation of man concluded the creative acts of God in the actual historical sequence as well as in the order of narration.[77]

If the normal conditions of rain were absolutely required, the normal conditions for human agriculture should also have been required. Conversely, if agricultural plants may live for a while without the hands of man under particular or extraordinary conditions, these plants could also live without rain for a while. M. J. Kruger says:

> Kline's proposal makes the mention of man in Genesis 2:5 entirely irrelevant. Would it make logical and coherent sense for the text to first assure the reader in verse 5 that man is a prerequisite for these plants to grow and then turn around in the very next verse and say that man after all is not really required? This is simply not what the Hebrew text tells us. Kline fails to account for the fact that Genesis 2:5 clearly offers two reasons for why there were no plants: rain *and* man.[78]

One must also take note that the second "deficiency" is "solved" not by any "normal" providential means but by the *supernatural creation* of man. The first "deficiency" is solved by the "mixing" of the mist of water with the ground ("and a mist was going up from the land and was watering the whole face of the ground," 2:6), whereas the second "deficiency" is solved by the "mixing" of the breathing of the Lord with the dust of the ground ("then the Lord God formed the man of dust from the ground and breathed into his nostrils the breath of life, and the man became a living creature," 2:7). Even if the first solution depended solely on normal providence, the second solution was certainly of a different nature. In order to have a fertile agricultural area (the garden of Eden), God at least created the cultivator in a supernatural way.[79]

Kline does not see a conflict between his theory and the creation of man after the plants because he excludes man from what he calls "ordinary providence." "With adequate natural irrigation already available, the mere preservation of vegetation does not require man's husbandry. But its full horticultural exploitation does."[80] When man is excluded from "normal" providential means, the Bible is approached with naturalistic and modern environmentalistic presuppositions.

God's plan for the providential care of at least some plants in the creation and especially in the garden of Eden certainly required the creation of man, not just the watering of the ground. The Lord provided a gardener: "The Lord God took the man and put him in the garden of Eden to work it and keep it" (2:15). When Kline adds that "the mention of man at this point need not be accounted for solely in terms of his services to the vegetable kingdom for he was not made for it but it for him,"[81] he does not solve the problem but only reinforces it. If the vegetable kingdom was made for man, how can the conditions of the existence of plants during the period man was not there yet be called normal or ordinary providence?

We may fully agree that "the mere preservation of vegetation does not require man's husbandry" (provided we do not call that preservation "ordinary providence," at least for the preservation of some plants on earth or in the garden, for the reasons just mentioned). But then we are back at square one and the problem related to the two "deficiencies" noticed in Genesis 2:5. Kruger adds:

> If Kline wishes to insist that Genesis 2:5 does apply to all plant life on the Earth, then he would have to also suggest that all the plants on the Earth require the cultivation of man (for we have already established above that man is just as much required as the rain). But, this faces two problems. First, this is contrary to the plain facts of nature because there are many plants that can exist without the help of man to cultivate the ground. Second, Kline would have to affirm that all plant life came upon the Earth after man. However, to any version of ancient Earth history this suggestion is absurd in the highest degree—particularly on their scheme man came millions of years after plants.[82]

Other possible interpretations of Genesis 2:5

Let us have a closer look at the text. The word *terem* in Genesis 2:5 may be taken as an adverb having the sense of "not yet," or functioning in Hebrew as a conjunction having the sense of "before."[83]

In the case of a *conjunction*, it is possible to translate Genesis 2:4b–6 the way the King James Version did: ". . .in the day that the Lord God made the earth and the heavens, and every plant of the field *before* it was in the earth, and every herb of the field *before* it grew: for the Lord God had not caused it to rain upon the earth, and there was not a man to till the ground. But there went up a mist from the earth, and watered the whole face of the ground." Calvin also translated it in a similar way.

This means that when God created every plant and herb of the field (or bush and small plant of the field, according to ESV), the normal conditions for growth and culture of these plants, as we know them today (rain and human agriculture), did not exist yet. *In spite of* these "deficiencies," God did actually create these plants. He created vegetation by His powerful Word, and then He miraculously preserved it without using ordinary means for a while, such as rain or human labour, which did not exist yet. Calvin understood the text precisely this way:

> But although he has before related that the herbs were created on the third day, yet it is not without reason that here again mention is made of them, in order that we may know that they were then produced, preserved, and propagated, *in a manner different from that which we perceive at the present day.* For herbs and trees are produced from seed; or grafts are taken from another root or they grow by putting forth shoots: in all this the industry and the hand of man are engaged. *But, at that time, the method was different:* God clothed the earth, not in the same manner as now (for there was no seed, no root, no plant, which might germinate), but each suddenly sprung into exis-

> tence at the command of God, and by the power of his word. They possessed durable vigour, so that they might stand by the force of their own nature,[84] and not by that quickening influence which is now perceived, not by the help of rain, not by the irrigation or culture of man; but *by the vapour with which God watered the earth.* For he excludes these two things, the rain whence the earth derives moisture, that it may retain its native sap; and human culture, which is the assistant of nature.[85]

If this is the meaning of this text, then it completely neutralizes Kline's interpretation and does not presuppose at all that plants were created only when normal conditions for their life were totally put in place; instead, the opposite is true. Genesis 2:5 is then in perfect harmony with the chronological order of the days of Genesis 1.

Other commentaries take the word *terem* according to its *adverbial* value with the meaning of "not yet," without necessarily concluding that all the plants of the earth were created only when normal conditions for their life existed. Genesis 2:5 possibly presents us a local situation, the project of an agricultural area, contrasting with the beauty of the garden of Eden where man would experience the special goodness of God. This passage is then understood in the context of the following verses, where God plants the garden of Eden and places man in it to cultivate it (see Gen. 2:8–15).

> The text is not dealing with a universal defect but highlights the placing of Adam in the garden. . . Even if there were a two-fold deficit, its reference is to the garden and not to the creation as a whole. . . Therefore, one ought not apply the reference to providence to the entire time of creation.[86]

> The only reason Kline sees ordinary providence as the only *modus operandi* is because he thinks Genesis 2:5 is referring to Day Three (Tuesday) in the creative process

> and thus applicable to all the Earth. . . However, Kline simply fails to realize that Genesis 2:5 is not speaking of Day Three (Tuesday) at all. As we have demonstrated above, Genesis 2:5 is only concerned with specific plants in the Garden of Eden and does not impact the plants spoken of in Day Three. Kline's accusation misses the point entirely due to his faulty exegesis of the text.[87]

The "bush[es] of the field" (2:5) and "the small plants of the field" (2:5) are not necessarily the same plants as those already created on the third day, i.e. "vegetation, plants yielding seed, and fruit trees bearing fruit" (1:11). Maybe these specific plants in Genesis 2:5, at least "the bush[es] of the field," are already created but do not produce buds or sprouts yet (which is the possible meaning of the word "spring up"). In any case, Genesis 2:5 would not be related to the third day but to the sixth day. The "earth" (*erets*) would refer to a large geographic area, whereas the "field" (*sadeh*) would refer to a more limited geographic area, a suitable place for agriculture.

Genesis 2:5 would not be telling us that no plants were created yet, but would explain why *agriculture* is not organized yet in the garden. It is because the two essential elements to agriculture (rain and cultivator) are absent. Even if it had not rained yet, the plants already created on the third day may have been preserved in an unknown supernatural way or by the mist or the streams of water, which came up from the earth and irrigated the whole surface of the ground (2:6). Besides, a plant may survive a few days without water.

> Although the growth of the shrubs and sprouting of the herbs are represented here as dependent upon the rain and the cultivation of the earth by man, we must not understand the words as meaning that there was neither shrub nor herb before the rain and dew, or before the creation of man, and so draw the conclusion that the creation of the plants occurred either after or contempora-

> neously with the creation of man, in direct contradiction to chap. i. 11, 12. The creation of the plants is not alluded to here at all, but simply the planting of the garden of Eden. The growing of the shrubs and sprouting of the herbs is different from the creation or first production of the vegetable kingdom, and relates to the growing and sprouting of the plants and germs which were called into existence by the creation, the natural development of the plants as it had steadily proceeded ever since the creation. This was dependent upon rain and human culture; their creation was not. Moreover, *the shrub and herb of the field* do not embrace the whole of the vegetable productions of the earth. It is not a fact that '*the field* is used in the second section in the same sense as *the earth* in the first'. [Sadeh] is not 'the widespread plain of the earth, the broad expanse of land,' but a field of arable land, soil fit for cultivation, which forms only a part of the 'earth' or 'ground.'[88]

Moreover, Genesis 2 focuses on man and on the very special place chosen for agriculture. Genesis 2 does not focus on the "deficiencies" but on the fact that, *in spite of* these "deficiencies" (no rain, no man to till the ground), God is free to miraculously plant and preserve a wonderful garden of Eden. This garden is watered by four rivers (no need to wait for rain) and God Himself made all kinds of trees grow out of the ground—trees that were pleasing to the eye and good for food (no need to wait for man tilling the ground).

The goodness of God towards man is abundant and does not depend at all on the natural conditions of growth of plants as we know them today. Man, the last creative work of God, receives on the sixth day a wonderful habitat, a garden that is not irrigated or preserved by rain, nor is it the fruit of his own working the ground. Before they undertook their work, man and woman had another reason to marvel at the power and the goodness of their Creator.

Thus, it is incorrect to conclude from Genesis 2:5 that originally all the plants of the earth were necessarily placed into "normal" conditions of growth and that they consequently needed a long time to grow or needed sun and rain as soon as they were created. It is even more fallacious, based on this verse alone, to stretch out the idea of "exclusive normal providence" to the whole of the creation week, including the light, which should have absolutely needed the sun for its existence. No matter whether one considers *terem* as being used in its adverbial or conjunctive sense, there is no reason to conclude that Genesis 2:5 should contradict the chronological sequence or the normal length of the days of Genesis 1.

The alleged principle drawn from Genesis 2:5 pushed to the absurd

Based on his understanding of Genesis 2:5, Kline formulated the thesis that *all* the created realities should have been preserved exclusively by ordinary providential means as we know and observe them today.

> The unargued presupposition of Gen. 2:5 is clearly that the divine providence was operating during the creation period through processes which any reader would recognize as normal in the natural world of his day.[89]

> Embedded in Gen. 2:5ff. is the principle that the *modus operandi* of the divine providence was the same during the creation period as that of ordinary providence at the present time.[90]

Kline applies "the *modus operandi* of the divine providence" he found in Genesis 2:5 to the whole creation week. The continents emerged from under the seas "by the ordinary process of evaporation" (third day). Plant life (product of the third day) flourished on the earth according to present natural law; this means it did not exist without the sun (product of the fourth day). Even the light (created on the first day) and the division of days and nights were not possible without the sun, according to this principle.

In a more recent article, Kline continues to apply this principle to other created things: to symbiotic situations where the survival of a particular kind of vegetation (third day) is dependent on the activity of animal life (fifth or sixth day), and even to cosmology. According to "normal" providential procedure, the earth came into existence (first day), not "by itself as a solitary sphere," but "as part of the cosmological process by which stars and their satellites originate" (fourth day). Kline's understanding of Genesis 2:5 and of its "presupposed principle" clearly contradicts the sequence and chronology of the literal interpretation of the creation days. Apparently one can find many things in just one (difficult) verse and can uphold them in a very categorical way.

Here is what Kline says to those who, contrary to him, understand the first and fourth days sequentially:

> And of course the existence of the earth itself on day one confronts the traditional approaches with a gigantic exception to normal providential procedure. For according to them the earth would have come into existence by itself as a solitary sphere, not as part of the cosmological process by which stars and their satellites originate, and it would have continued alone, suspended in a spatial void (if we may so speak) for the first three days of creation. All the vast universe whose origin is narrated on day four would then be younger (even billions of years younger) than the speck in space called earth. So much for the claimed harmony of the narrative sequence of Genesis 1 with scientific cosmology.[91]
>
> Our argument is that Genesis 2:5–6 informs us that the mode of divine providence during the creation period was *ordinary* rather than *extraordinary*. This rules out the possibility that the daylight was caused by a supernatural or nonsolar light source for the first three days, thus

forcing us to view the fourth day as a temporal recapitulation and the days in general as being nonsequential.[92]

J. A. Pipa has pointed out the logical fallacy of such a reasoning:

> Dr. Kline's reasoning involves a logical fallacy. One may not prove the truth of a universal from the truth of a particular. For example, one may not argue that because many of the best professional baseball players are from Latin America all the best professional baseball players are from Latin America. Therefore, particular evidence of ordinary providence during creation, may not be used to prove universal ordinary providence during creation.[93]

The presence of ordinary providence during the creation week does not disprove the possibility of extraordinary providence. M. J. Kruger also makes some pertinent points:

> God was certainly using a *mixture* of both extraordinary and ordinary providence during the Creation Week. Extraordinary providence would only be unnecessary if God created everything at one time. It is only when every component of the complex universe is in place that it functions without the help of God's extraordinary intervention. Whether it is the balance of gravity in our intricate solar system or the complex interdependence of the Earth's ecosystems, it is essential that all parts be in place in order for them to operate effectively. But even Kline does not suggest in his "framework hypothesis" that all things were created simultaneously, thus he too must posit certain acts of extraordinary providence intermingled with ordinary providence during the creation process. The only way in which Kline can maintain a *purely* naturalistic and ordinary creation process is to suggest that God used some evolutionary mechanism. This would entail a Deistic view of God which says that God simply

got the proverbial "ball" rolling and does not intervene in *any* sort of extraordinary manner. But the Scriptures clearly reject such a Deistic view of God.[94]

Kline wants to be consistent with his interpretation of Genesis 2:5; therefore, he must argue that the earth could not have existed without the normal cosmological process by which stars and their satellites originate. In other words, the earth created on the first day and formed on the second and third days could not have been created and developed without the sun and the stars created on the fourth day. And where is this written? All this construction would be included in an alleged comprehensive principle drawn from just one verse: Genesis 2:5. A sequential interpretation of Genesis 1 would contradict both Genesis 2:5 and the so-called "scientific cosmology." One wonders which is more important for the framework proponents: Genesis 2:5 or the so-called "scientific cosmology"?

This idea of exclusive normal providence and of the coexistence of the earth and the lights during the time of their creation is contrary to the Word of God for the following reasons:

- Genesis 1:1–2 says that God created heaven and earth, and that the Spirit was hovering over the mass of water. The action of the Spirit on this mass of water does not just describe normal providential process, but a creative act or an extraordinary providential act preparing a new creative act.

- Once this mass of water is created, according to the framework theory, it should have been preserved and modified only by normal process of divine providence. On the contrary, Genesis 1:6–8 says that God created "an expanse" between the waters to separate waters from waters. The waters here are not created; they are just *separated*. They are separated by the creation of this "expanse." The events described on the second day in Genesis 1:6–8 present a divine creative act ("And God made the expanse," 1:7) and this act modified an existing reality in a *supernatural* way ("to separate waters from waters").

- Once the expanse is created, according to the framework theory, it should have been preserved and modified only by normal processes of divine providence. On the contrary, Genesis 1:14–18 says that God created the lights (sun, moon, stars) "in the expanse." The events described on the fourth day in Genesis 1:14–18 present a divine creative act ("And God made the two great lights. . . and the stars," 1:16) and this act modified in a *supernatural* way the "inside" of the existing expanse.

When we take seriously the *events* described in Genesis 1, we clearly see the following chronological order: the creation of the waters, then the creation of the expanse, which separated these waters, then the creation of the lights, which were put in this expanse. This chronological order is inescapable unless one denies that the expanse really separated the waters[95] and that the lights were really put into the expanse. In order to maintain the framework theory, one must deny that these creative acts really happened the way the Bible reveals it. It is too bad for the so-called "scientific cosmology" (as if there were only one[96]), but according to the description of the events in Genesis 1, it is impossible that the water (the beginning of the earth), the expanse, the sun, and the stars were formed together as part of a long "cosmological process."

When the Lord commanded the lights to come into existence, the expanse already existed and was already named. "And God said, 'Let there be lights in the expanse of the heavens'" (1:14). And when those lights were created, the earth was already there, ready to be lit by them, unless one *denies* that the Lord really said, "and let them be lights in the expanse of the heavens to give light upon the earth" (1:15). The framework theory really reaches here the limits of the absurd. The alleged principle of normal providential means does not stand in Genesis 1 any more than in Genesis 2:5. In fact, the whole thesis based on this strange interpretation of Genesis 2:5 crumbles in light of Genesis 1.

Here is a last example of this alleged principle pushed to the absurd. We know that the man was created before the woman (Gen. 2:18–23; 1 Cor. 11:8–9; 1 Tim. 2:13). How would the man have been able to live according to God's plan without the woman, only by "normal" providential means? God Himself made a wise judgment on the situation: "It is not good that the man should be alone" (2:18). To remedy the situation, God needed to operate not by ordinary providential means nor even by extraordinary providential means but by a new supernatural creative act. The Lord caused Adam to fall into a deep sleep; He took one of his ribs and made a woman from the rib. The fact that God did not always use only "normal" providential means to preserve and maintain His created works is again indisputable. Genesis 2 confirms it.

Theological implications

As a conclusion to our evaluation of the evidence from Genesis 2:5, Frank Walker's remarks are relevant here:

> More to the point, we must question Kline's assumption that God's *modus operandi* during the creation week was ordinary providence. It is doubtful that this can be established from Genesis 2:5. Genesis 2 deals specifically with the creation of man and his environment, enlarging upon the brief account given in chapter 1. As we study it, we have to keep in mind that man was unique among the rest of creation. He alone was formed in the image of God and, therefore, able to love God and walk with him. He alone was given a mandate to exercise dominion over all things. He alone had the responsibility to tend and keep the Garden of Eden. *The fact that man was responsible for his environment as vice-regent of God entails ordinary providence.* Adam had to observe meteorological conventions

and learn how to irrigate the Garden in dry spells. Note is taken of this in Genesis 2 because *the creation of man brought about a radical change in the way God exercised his government of the world.* During the first five days God ruled the world entirely by extraordinary providence. There is no evidence in Genesis 1 of anything else. But with the creation of man (to whom the Lord gave a fair amount of responsibility) ordinary providence was put into effect. Genesis 2:5 must be understood in relation to man's unique place and responsibility. Indeed, this seems to be the only acceptable possibility when we take into account the topical recapitulation of Genesis 2:4–7.[97]

5

Genesis 2:19 [98]

It has been said by M. Futato that "a straightforward reading of Genesis 2:19 puts Genesis 2:4–25 in conflict with a chronological reading of Genesis 1:1–2:3, where the animals were formed before the man (Gen. 1:24–27)."[99] According to this view, Genesis 1 teaches that the creation of the animals happened before the creation of man, whereas Genesis 2:19, understood in a simple, literal way, presents the opposite sequence. But why should we see problems where the framework proponents themselves do not see problems? For example, Kline says that "the creation of man concluded the creative acts of God in the actual historical sequence as well as in the order of narration."[100] This perfectly fits with what is revealed in Genesis 1. The framework proponents do not see any problem, on this point, in the temporal sequence of the fifth and sixth days of Genesis 1.

How, then, should we understand Genesis 2:19? This text seems to say that God created Adam, then all the animals of the fields, then all the birds, then Eve. But of course it is not what the framework proponents understand, since they believe that man and woman were created last. Then how do we harmonize Genesis 2:19 with this idea? We may simply understand the tense of the verb "to form" as a pluperfect into a sequential narrative: "So out of the ground the

Lord God *had formed* every beast of the field and every bird of the heavens." The creation of the animals is then understood as preceding the creation of Adam, without forcing the grammatical meaning of the text.[101] M. Ross, a framework proponent, is quite willing to concede it and calls this an "inclusion" that simply prepares the account of the creation of Eve.[102] Therefore, there is no contradiction between Genesis 2:19 and the chronological order of Genesis 1.

Besides, even if everything is not chronological in Genesis 2, this does not imply that Genesis 1 must be nonchronological, especially when the Holy Spirit gives us temporal indications as strong as "day one," "evening and morning," "second day," "evening and morning," "third day," etc. There is no need to confuse us with an alleged problem in Genesis 2.[103] If man was actually created after the animals, then the chronological sequence of the fifth and the sixth days of Genesis is correct.

In conclusion to this first part, the objections raised against the literal interpretation do not stand in the light of a serious study of the text. In order to sustain the hypothesis of the framework interpretation and of other figurative variants, one must begin to see problems that do not exist in Genesis 1 or between Genesis 1 and Genesis 2. Thus, we have not been convinced to abandon the classic understanding of the days of creation. On the contrary, the literal understanding of the days of creation perfectly fits the revelation of the work of creation in the space of six days as found in Genesis.

II

THE FRAMEWORK INTERPRETATION IS PROBLEMATIC

1

"Literal"

Some maintain that the figurative interpretation is not an allegorical interpretation of the text but a literal one. By that, they mean that the figurative understanding is the real meaning that the sacred writer wanted to communicate.[104] We can appreciate the desire to present the true meaning of Scripture. Nevertheless, in order to avoid confusion, we should keep the word "literal" for those who understand the days of creation in their literal meaning. It is clear that, according to the framework theory, the days or the week must be taken in a *figurative* or *metaphorical* sense.

H. Blocher does not hesitate to describe the classic interpretation as "literal," as opposed to the "literary" interpretation, which he promotes. We have no problem with him, at least on this point. As for stating whether the framework is the correct interpretation or not, this is precisely the subject of the debate. Therefore, we may continue to call the traditional interpretation "literal." It is precisely this interpretation that has been very largely sustained in church history until the work of Charles Lyell (geology) and Charles Darwin (biology).[105]

2

The Structure In Two Triads

The framework proponents detect in the first chapter of Genesis a literary structure skilfully written, presenting a two-triad parallel. According to N. H. Ridderbos:

> A. Noordtzij points out that "the six days of Genesis 1 are obviously intended as the sum of two triduums which consequently reveal a clearly pronounced parallelism, while the total arrangement is intended to place in bold relief the surpassing glory of man who attains his true destiny in the sabbath." In this connection he declares: "Given this plan of the creation account we may infer meanwhile that the author consciously used days and nights, evenings and mornings, as a literary framework."[106]

Following in the footsteps of Noordtzij and Ridderbos, Irons and Kline say:

> The first exegetical argument for the framework interpretation begins with the observation that the days form a framework consisting of two parallel triads. The first triad (days 1–3) deals with the *creation kingdoms*, while the

> second triad (days 4–6) deals with the *creature kings* who exercise dominion over those kingdoms.[107]

Differences exist on how to classify the two triads, though. Others prefer the dual "forming" and "filling" themes for the two triads, corresponding to the two "deficiencies" mentioned in Genesis 1:2: "The earth was without form and void." M. Ross, for example, says:

> Days one through three give form to the earth, overcoming the 'formless-ness' identified in Genesis 1:2; days four through six fill these various realms, filling the 'void' identified in Genesis 1:2.[108]

H. Blocher and others have a similar approach. In any case, the parallel would be between day one and day four (the light and the lights), between day two and day five (the sky and the flying animals; also the sea and the sea creatures), and between day three and day six (the land and the land animals; also the plants and man). Additionally, Futato observes that there are four creative acts in days one to three, and four in days four to six, with two on day three and two on day six. The first triad concludes with vegetation and the second with man, introducing the two-fold theme picked up in Genesis 2.[109]

It does not matter which approach is chosen; all the proponents of the framework theory conclude that this literary device is a strong argument in favour of a figurative interpretation of the days of creation. According to them, the two-triad structure points to the idea that Genesis 1 is intended to teach us a theological meaning as opposed to a chronological sequence of the days of creation. The author did not intend to present a chronological account of the creative acts. He wanted to present the creative acts in a thematic format, somewhat like a photo album arranged according to a thematic order.[110] Unfortunately, this literary argument is often repeated from one commentary to another without taking the time to scrutinize its validity and to carefully examine the literary details.

A parallel between the first day and the fourth day?[111]

Let us examine the alleged parallel between the first day and the fourth day. It is true that some elements in the triads are related to each other, but we must take a closer look. The framework interpretation says that there is a parallelism between two triads (between the first three days and the following three days). Each day of the creation week is introduced by a divine announcement—"And God said"—providing a framework for each day. Within each day, the author gives one snapshot of God's creative work on the first, second, fourth, and fifth days, or two snapshots on the third and sixth days. The eight creative acts are evenly divided into two parallel units of three days presenting four events. In this context, the creation of the light on the first day is parallel to the creation of the lights on the fourth day. These two triads are supposed to have as themes the "*forming*" and the "*filling,*" or the "*kingdoms*" and "*kings,*" and that would correspond to the two "deficiencies" indicated in Genesis 1:2: "The earth was without form and void."

The first problem with this view is that the creation of the light is not the only creative act that happened on the first day. The heavens and the earth were also created on that very first day. Some regard Genesis 1:1 as the title of the whole narrative of creation. But this is objectionable because, on that supposition, there would be no account whatsoever of the original and immediate creation. This includes the creation of the heavens and their invisible order of things, not mentioned anywhere else in the chapter. This also includes the creation of the waters, which are described in verse 2 as an existing reality. Then in the second verse the author describes the original condition of the earth. Irons and Kline, as well as other framework proponents, agree with that when they say that the creation of the heavens and the earth is "the absolute beginning" and not a summary heading.[112] Nevertheless, they are inconsistent when they limit the comparison of the first and the fourth days to the light and the lights. They exclude the creation of the heavens and the earth from the framework.

Another problem with this view is that Genesis 1:2 does not mention two but at least *three* "deficiencies": the earth was formless, empty, and *dark*.[113] "Darkness was over the face of the deep" (1:2). It is even possible to see in Genesis 1:2 *four* "problems," including the *waters*, that need to be resolved by God before the earth can be a habitable place for man to live.[114] From the start, we see that the "two-triad" structure, if based on Genesis 1:2, seems shaky. When God created the universe, He formed, filled, and lit it. One should not reduce God's creative acts to a dual reality ("forming and filling," or "kingdoms and kings") in order to satisfy one's desire to find "literary devices." This reduction may well impoverish our understanding of God's manifold wisdom displayed in His creative acts.

For which one of these three or four "problems" mentioned in Genesis 1:2 is the first day a remedy? Some framework proponents say it is for the formless earth. The first day is supposed to be part of the "forming" triad. In fact, it would be better to understand the creation of light as solving the third "deficiency," the "problem" of darkness.

For the fourth day associated with the "filling" triad, one really wonders which reality created on the first day the lights "fill" (especially if the heavens and the earth are excluded). The lights also have the function of giving light on the earth, so that they remedy the "darkness" deficiency but not that of "emptiness," when compared with the first day. If the lights have any "filling" role, it is "in the expanse" (1:14), where the Lord put them. The correspondence in language is quite explicit. This expanse is not mentioned at all on the first day, but is found five times on the second day and three times on the fourth day. Therefore, the fourth day would be parallel to the second day, when the expanse is created, and not to the first day.

For those who propose the kingdoms/kings themes, the problem seems to be solved, since the greater light was made to "rule the day" and the lesser light "to rule the night" (1:16). But then the parallel between the two days becomes more confused. It is not a parallel between two creative acts: "Let there be *light*" (1:2) and "Let there be *lights*" (1:14). The text does not say that the lights are made to rule over the light; it says they were created "to rule over the day and over the night" (1:18).

Of course day and night appear on the very first day. God separated the light from the darkness and called the light "day" and the darkness he called "night" (1:5). Likewise, on the fourth day He created the lights "to separate the light from the darkness" (1:18). There is an obvious similarity in the function of light and darkness on the first day and in one of the functions of the lights on the fourth day. The question is: Does that mean that the parallel is between a king and a kingdom? This is not the case. The parallel is between *two different ways* of separating days and nights. The parallel is between light and darkness separating day and night (from day one to day three), and lights governing and separating day and night (from day four onward). We believe this approach gives a better recognition to the main acts of creation on both days, namely light and lights, without forcing the text to fit into a neat literary device.

We conclude that the parallel between the first day and the fourth day proposed by the framework theory is not accurate.

A parallel between the second day and the fifth day?

Let us now examine the alleged parallel between the second day and the fifth day. On the fifth day, aquatic creatures are created to fill or govern the water, and birds are created to fill or govern the heavens created on the second day, thus confirming the two-triad structure. A closer look, however, reveals some major problems. First, on the second day there is one divine announcement with two commands for one creative activity, the creative activity being the expanse: "And God said, 'Let there be an expanse in the midst of the waters, and let it separate the waters from the waters'" (1:6). In contrast, its supposedly corresponding day has one divine announcement with two commands for two creative activities, those being the sea creatures and the birds: "And God said, 'Let the waters swarm with swarms of living creatures, and let birds fly above the earth across the expanse of the heavens'" (1:20).

In addition, on the fifth day the aquatic animals are in fact given the mandate to "fill" the waters, but are these waters really those of the second day? Actually, the waters existing on the second day were already created on the first day: "And the Spirit of God was hovering over the face of the waters" (1:2). If one is to make a parallel between the second day and the fifth day, why not then between the first day and the fifth day? Moreover, the creative work accomplished on the second day is the creation of the *expanse*, which separates these waters in two parts, not the creation of the waters: "Let there be an expanse. . . And God made the expanse. . . And God called the expanse Heaven" (1:6–8). It is difficult to see a strict correspondence with any of the two creative acts on the fifth day: "Let the waters swarm with swarms of living creatures and let birds fly above the earth. . ." (1:20).

The "waters above" will not contain the fish anyway. These fish have certainly not received the mandate to fill the water in the atmosphere (vapour), or the water on planets or in interstellar space, or the waters at the outer edge of the universe.[115] These "waters above" appearing on the second day apparently do not have any corresponding "inhabitants" created on the fifth day. As for the "waters under the expanse" appearing on the second day, they need first to be better "formed." The dry land must appear before the "waters under the expanse" can receive fish, whales, and sea animals. God gathers these waters only on the third day, and it is only after having gathered them that He calls them "seas" (1:10).

In this context, it is noticeable that the fish are not "fish of the water" but "fish of the sea" (1:26, 28); they will fill "the waters in the seas" (1:22). Their habitat has been made on the third day and not on the second day. When one seeks a correspondence with the fish of the fifth day, one will find it on the third day instead. Irons and Kline mistakenly say that "on day two, [the author] narrates the creation of the sky and sea kingdoms in the following order: the sky is created first, then the seas."[116] This error is misleading, especially when it is also stated in the chart illustrating the parallel between the two triads.[117]

What about the birds also created on the fifth day? What do they fill? We tend to say that they fill the heavens. Irons and Kline declare:

> The parallel day-frame in the second triad (Day 5) records the creation of the corresponding kings in reverse order: the creation of the kings of the sea-kingdom is narrated first, then that of the winged creatures to rule over the sky-kingdom.[118]

It is true that the birds are really called "birds of the heavens" (or sky) (1:26, 28), but is it the whole sky of the second day? The expanse created on the second day and called "heavens" includes the whole interstellar space since it contains the sun, the moon, and the stars. "Let there be lights *in* the expanse of the heavens" (1:14). It would be asking too much of the birds to fill these "heavens" or rule over them. Moreover, verse 20 says (my translation), "Let the birds fly on the earth, on the surface of the expanse of the heavens." This means that from the perspective of an observer on earth, the birds fly *under* the heavens. Their habitat (nesting, feeding, etc.) is more the earth than the heavens. Accordingly, the text says, "Let the birds multiply *on the earth*" (1:22). The area they have to fill is not so much the "heavens" as the "earth," which appeared on the third day. Again, if one wants to find a parallel based on the duality habitats/inhabitants, it would be better to connect the fifth day with the third one. N. H. Ridderbos admits that the parallelism is strained but does not take the problem seriously:

> It must be granted that the birds (vv. 20, 22) are also associated with the earth, and the fishes (v. 22) with the seas, that is, with entities which arose on the third day and not on the second. But this must not be given much weight. . . We may not expect rigid classification from the author.[119]

What about the kingdoms/kings approach? What about the "governing" function of the fish and birds? Some proponents of the framework theory suggest that the ruling of the animals over their respective kingdoms can be deduced from their mandate to "be fruitful and multiply and fill the waters in the seas, and let birds multiply on the earth" (1:22). This deduction, however, is not based on any clear proof text. The mandate to "be fruitful and multiply and fill" is not the same as the mandate to govern.

The mandate to rule or govern is specifically given to the lights on the fourth day, "to rule over the day and over the night" (1:18), and to man on the sixth day, to "have dominion over the fish of the sea and over the birds of the heavens and over every living thing that moves on the earth" (1:28). While having the function "to rule over the day and over the night" (1:18), the lights certainly do not have the mandate to multiply!

On the other hand, man received the mandate to *both* "fill the earth *and* subdue it" (1:28). Why did God bother adding this second command to man and not to the animals? It would have been easy for an author who is fond of literary devices to be more precise here about the fifth day. The reason for this silence is simply because filling and subduing are two different roles. Man's kingship is extended to the "sea kingdom" and the "air kingdom." Otherwise how could he "have dominion over the fish *of the sea* and over the birds *of the heavens*" (1:26)? It does not follow that man had to multiply in order to fill the sea and the air. Furthermore, the man-king did not have to "compete" with the alleged "fish-kings" and "birds-kings" in the original "very good" creation. According to Genesis 1, there is no other king on the whole earth than man and woman created in the image of God. The task of subduing God's creation in the name of the great King is closely related to being created in the image of God—a privilege that is not given to any other creature, neither the fish nor the birds. "Then God said, 'Let us make man in our image, after our likeness. And let them have dominion over the fish of the sea and over the birds of the heavens and over the livestock and over all the earth and over every creeping thing that creeps on the earth.'" (1:26). The supposed kingly office of the fish, birds, and beasts of the earth is a pure theological fabrication that is totally baseless and contrary to Scripture. Consequently, the kingdoms/kings theme of the two-triad structure does not work any better than the forming/filling theme.

Thus, the proposed parallel between the second day and the fifth day is not accurate.

A parallel between the third day and the sixth day?

One more alleged parallel needs to be examined. According to the framework theory, the third day and the sixth day are supposed to be parallel as well. The animals and man are created to govern or fill the land. It is certainly true that the land animals will live on the earth and fill it, as well as the man and the woman who are called to multiply on the earth. But what about the "governing" function of the land animals? The same remarks as in the previous paragraph apply here. The exclusive kingship of man on the land is even more obvious. *Both* man and land animals have to *fill* the same habitat. "Let the earth bring forth living creatures according to their kinds" (1:24). Likewise, to man God said, "Fill the earth" (1:28). However, *only* man is required to "*subdue* the earth" (1:28). No such thing is said about the land animals.

It is true that there is some correspondence between the third day and the sixth day. There is an obvious parallel between the creating of dry land and the creating of land animals. Nevertheless, it is also possible to see a correspondence between the fifth day and the sixth day, or between the first part of the sixth day and its second part. For the man (sixth day) has to rule over the fish and over the birds (fifth day), as well as over the land animals (beginning of the sixth day). Why should we arbitrarily choose to underline one parallel and not the others? God's creative works are all interconnected. For this reason, it is easy to find connections between different works made on different days. We must be careful, however, not to choose (or even imagine) some of these connections and forget others just because we want to find a two-triad structure in the text.

Moreover, it is very difficult to say that the animals and the man of the sixth day will "inhabit" or "fill" the vegetation of the third day. A new theme other than "filling" or "governing" needs to be introduced in order to maintain the triad, namely, the theme of "food" or "eating." The plants will be the food provision for the land inhabitants: "Behold, I have given you every plant yielding seed that is on the face of all the earth, and every tree with seed in its fruit. You shall have them for food" (1:29). Even the birds were given plants for food (1:30), thus making a new parallel between the third day and the fifth day, instead of the sixth. Besides, does this vegetation remedy the formlessness or the emptiness of Genesis 1:2? "Let the earth *sprout* vegetation. . ." (1:11). This corresponds more to the "filling" role than to the "forming," although the plants are created on the third day, in the first "triad."

Futato admits that the parallel between the third day and the sixth day is strained: "It may seem that the parallelism breaks down at the end, because vegetation and mankind may not seem like much of a parallel."[120] To circumvent this "breakdown," Futato maintains that "when one recalls the twofold focus on vegetation and humanity in Genesis 2:4–25, the parallelism becomes evident."[121] Irons and Kline add:

> The dual thematic focus established by the parallel third and sixth day-frames sets the stage for Genesis 2:4–25, which resumes and expands upon this twofold theme of vegetation and man. Moses places two creative acts on Day 3 and Day 6, while all the other days contain only one fiat, which strengthens the connection between vegetation and man, thus preparing for the subsequent narrative which would explain that connection in greater detail (Gen. 2:4–25).[122]

This seems to presuppose that the vegetation created on the third day of Genesis 1 is the same as the vegetation and trees that God planted in the garden of Eden in Genesis 2. It appears, however, that the vegetation planted in the garden of Eden was created not on the third day but on the sixth day, after the creation of Adam: "Then the Lord God formed the man. . ., and the man became a living creature. And the Lord God planted a garden in Eden, in the east, and there he put the man whom he had formed. And out of the ground the Lord God made to spring up every tree that is pleasant to the sight and good for food" (2:7–8). McCabe also makes this interesting comment:

> Theologically, it is clear that Adam's probation in Genesis 2 is related to the vegetation of the Garden of Eden, in particular the tree of knowledge of good and evil. Nevertheless, the connection between man and vegetation in Genesis 2 is not the same thing as the connection between land animals and dry land. In order to have a consistent parallel [between Day 3 and Day 6], it should follow that man was formed out of vegetation, as the animals were formed out of dry land. In reality, this example is a comparison of apples and oranges.[123]

Lastly, nothing is created on the sixth day to fill the seas gathered on the third day. Once again, the alleged parallel between the third day and the sixth day is not precise.

In conclusion, a closer examination of the so-called "two-triad" structure reveals that the literary framework itself is very shaky. It becomes clear that this two-triad structure is not textually based but has been superimposed on the text. This alleged literary form of Genesis cannot be a solid basis for questioning, let alone denying the true historical reality of the days of creation.

Three "problems" structuring the six days?

Other theologians perceive literary structures in Genesis 1 that are different from the two triads. Interestingly, W. R. Godfrey detects in Genesis 1:2 three "problems," instead of two, that need to be solved before the earth can be a habitable place for man to live. "God, then, faces three obstacles to people living on the earth. First, the world was formless and empty. . . Second, the earth was dark. Third, waters covered the earth."[124]

One wonders how he counts three problems and not four. Godfrey does not explain why he considers "formless and empty" as only one problem, whereas other proponents of the figurative view have sustained that these are the two main "deficiencies" of Genesis 1:2 that are solved in the rest of the account. The threefold problem he suggests is convenient for his analysis of the literary structure of the days of creation, where a fourth "problem" called "formless" would not fit very well.

> God solves the problem of darkness in one day [day one]. He solves the problem of water covering the earth in two days (days two and three). Then he solves the problem of an empty world in three days (days four, five, and six). This progression of days is a way of emphasizing the importance of what is done to fill the earth since God gives more time to it.[125]

This view differs from the classic two-triad structure. Godfrey explains the two triads proposed by Irons and Kline ("kingdoms and kings") but admits that this insight has limits. On the one hand, he says that Genesis 1 has an intricate literary structure; on the other hand, he suggests that "the lack of exact correspondence at this point is not a major problem, however, since Hebrew literary structure often artfully varies forms so that they are not exactly balanced."[126] It seems that each proponent of the figurative view explains differently the "intricate" and "precise" literary structure of Genesis 1 and is prepared to make concessions called "artful varieties of forms. . . not exactly balanced" (Godfrey), or to say that "we may not expect rigid classification from the author" (Ridderbos), or that "it may seem that the parallelism breaks down at the end" (Futato), when the text does not exactly correspond to the theory.

Godfrey's insight on the relationship between Genesis 1:2 and days two and three is interesting and partly contradicts the two-triad structure. Considering the fact that his understanding of Genesis 1:2 is critical for his figurative view, it is important to analyze in more detail his literary pattern. Godfrey says:

> The point of Genesis 1:2 is that the earth God had brought into being was not yet a habitable place for the creature with whom God would have a covenantal relationship. God will act to form and arrange the world as a proper dwelling place for his image bearers. Genesis 1:2 is critical for understanding the rest of the creation narrative because the three elements that rendered the earth uninhabitable for humanity are dealt with one at a time in God's subsequent acts of creation. These problems are a key to understanding what God is revealing about the meaning of creation in Genesis 1.[127]

Godfrey is correct when he says that days two and three (at least day three) solve the problem of the waters on the earth. But is it the only "problem" they solve? Did God deal with those problems only "one at a time"? The focus of day two is not the water but the creation of the expanse in the heavens. All God's activities on that day are related to this expanse. "And God said. . . and God made. . . and God called" (1:6–8). Moreover, even though God does not declare anything "good" on that day, the creation of the expanse and the separation of the waters in two parts are clearly established: "And it was so" (1:7).

These divine activities do not exactly solve the problem of the waters on the earth. They primarily solve the problem of the formlessness of the world. On the second day God gives form and order in the heavens. As for the third day, God certainly solves the problem of the waters on the earth, but He also solves the problem of lack of food, which is not specifically mentioned in Genesis 1:2 but may be related to the problem of "emptiness."[128] Even though the problem of waters is solved and a sizeable piece of land is now dry, it is clear that the earth could not be inhabited by man as long as there was no food supply. We must be careful not to limit God's creative activities on the second and third days to solving only one "problem." The "engineering" of a habitat perfectly suitable for man is more complex than a literary device. These remarks also apply to the two-triad structure of the framework view.

The fourth problem that Godfrey sees for the traditional interpretation ("this view cannot easily account for the absence of the statement 'And God saw that it was good' in day two"[129]) is irrelevant. Godfrey explains this absence from a literary point of view (days two and three are taken together, together they answer one of the problems mentioned in Genesis 1:2). The literary structure of the text does not exclude the fact that God may really create something on one day and complete its shaping on a following day.

On the second day, God created the expanse and separated the waters. The text confirms that this expanse and this separation are established: "And it was so" (1:7). Nevertheless, the expanse needs to receive the "lights in the expanse" on the fourth day before "God saw that it was good" on the fourth day (1:18). In the same way, the waters under the heavens need to be gathered together into one place before "God saw that it was good" on the third day (1:12). From one day to the next, God progressively creates, forms, fills, etc., one step at a time, according to His sovereign will and pleasure. He does not need to see anything good on the second day, considering the fact that what He created on that day is established, and that more things need to be done in the expanse and with the waters. The "traditional" interpretation can easily account for the absence of the statement "And God saw that it was good" in day two.

Godfrey's figurative interpretation (the days of creation are only a pattern for man to follow, and not a real chronological description of God's creative activities) is partly based on the way he sees how the sixth day is connected to Genesis 1:2 and to the literary structure of the whole week.

> The commission to multiply is the occasion for further description of the function of man: fill the earth, subdue it, and rule over it. This threefold mandate given to man is critical not only for understanding the work of man on earth but also to seeing the structure and meaning of Genesis 1 as a whole. These three elements of man's responsibility correspond to the three problems of Genesis 1:2 and to the ways in which God dealt with them. Man is to rule over the earth in a way analogous to God's sovereignty over the darkness. . . Man is to subdue the earth in a way analogous to the way God subdued the waters. Man is to fill the earth with his offspring in a way analogous to the way God filled creation with creature.[130]

This analogy between man's work and God's work is very important for Godfrey, especially for his understanding of the days of creation.[131] Yet the whole structure (and meaning) he sees in Genesis 1 is very difficult to maintain. First, did man really receive a "threefold" mandate? In Genesis 1:28, five different verbs are used to describe his mandate: "Be fruitful and multiply and fill the earth and subdue it and have dominion over [the animals]." It is possible to claim that man received a twofold (children and work), a fourfold, or even a fivefold mandate, according to the combination of the verbs that are chosen. Godfrey's choice seems arbitrary, especially considering the fact that subduing and ruling are similar mandates, as much as being fruitful, multiplying, and filling the earth are similar mandates. Secondly, does the content of these mandates really correspond to the problems mentioned in Genesis 1:2?

The analogy that Godfrey sees between God's sovereignty over the darkness and man's dominion over the earth (or more precisely over the animals according to verses 26 and 28) is very difficult to understand. God is certainly sovereign over the light, but He is as much sovereign over the expanse, the waters, the dry land, the vegetation, the lights, the birds, the fish, and the land animals. Any "problem" solved by God's sovereign creative works on any of the six days could be arbitrarily considered analogous to man's dominion over the animals in order to "fit" the structure we want to impose on the text. A mandate given to man that would be specifically analogous to the divine activities performed in order to solve the problem of darkness should include some sort of human dominion over the light, the sun, the moon, the stars, and some sort of governance over the alternation of days and nights. No such things are mentioned in Genesis 1:28.

In the same way, it is also difficult to see that "man is to subdue the earth in a way analogous to the way God subdued the waters" on days two and three. God subdued the waters first by creating the expanse and by separating the waters, then by gathering the waters under the heavens together into one place. Man's alleged "analogous" working activity is to subdue the earth. What does this analogy mean? Man has not received any specific mandate to subdue the expanse or the waters above the expanse. Again, the choice of analogy seems arbitrary.

Just as for the two-triad structure, the literary structure suggested by Godfrey is not entirely textually based but has been superimposed on the text. This alleged literary form of Genesis 1 cannot be a solid basis for affirming that the days of creation are only a pattern for man to follow, and not a real chronological description of God's creative activities.

Other possible literary structures

J. B. Jordan suggests another literary structure in Genesis 1. He proposes a *chiasm* structure of the seven days (the first day responds to the seventh, the second to the sixth, the third to the fifth, and the fourth day plays a pivotal role at the centre). This form is frequently found in the Bible, and here it apparently reinforces the literal interpretation of the days of creation.[132] His suggestion is not totally convincing but would need to be studied more. One must be careful not to force the text to fit into imposed or imagined categories.[133]

Others have found the following structure, which repeats itself in the days of creation: First the divine speech ("And God said"), then the fiat or command ("Let there be"), then the fulfilment ("And it was so"), then the judgment ("And God saw that it was good"), and finally, the temporal conclusion ("And there was evening and there was morning: the *n*th day"). This obvious pattern is interesting and can be easily observed, except that "this arrangement is not consistently carried through for each of the days," as E. J. Young has observed. He concludes:

> Hence, it would seem that *the primary interest* of the writer was not a schematic classification or arrangement of material. His primary concern was to relate *how God created* the heaven and the earth.[134]

The most obvious and simple pattern of the text is still the "six plus one" structure—six days of creation followed by a seventh day consecrated to holy rest and blessed by the Lord. Exodus 20:8–11 and 31:17 emphasize the importance of this temporal pattern that must serve as model for man to imitate during his week of work and rest.

3

False Dilemmas

A refined literary composition vs the literal meaning

Let us suppose that Moses wrote Genesis 1 in a highly stylized literary form, and let us suppose that the two triads are perfectly parallel. What does that prove? Why should a refined literary composition exclude the literal meaning? Young rightly says, "A schematic disposition of the material in Genesis one does not prove, nor does it even suggest, that the days are to be taken in a non-chronological sense."[135]

The framework proponents reason in a strange way. They suggest that the more a text has a refined literary form, the less probable it contains a chronological order. Since Genesis 1 is written in a skilfully constructed literary form, it is more likely that the events recorded are not in a chronological order. How can Genesis 1 be *both* well-written *and* chronological? Since the author has a carefully crafted style, we suspect that the text contains a hidden figurative meaning. For example, H. Blocher says:

> We discerned a composite literary genre, skilfully composed. We admired its author as a wise man, supremely

> able in the art of arranging material and very fond of manipulating numbers, particularly the number seven. From such a writer the plain, straightforward meaning, as in two-dimensional prose, would be most surprising when he is setting out the pattern of seven days. From such a writer you would expect the sort of method which is discerned by the "artistic" interpretation.[136]

> The more it appears that the biblical writer used a stereotype from his cultural milieu in presenting the creation in the form of a week, the less likely is it that he limited himself to transcribing a chronological sequence.[137]

When Blocher speaks about "the plain, straightforward meaning, as in two-dimensional prose," this way of writing seems to have a clear negative connotation.[138] But where does this idea come from? Jean-Marc Berthoud criticizes Blocher on this point. Berthoud says:

> What difficulty would it be for [the Author of the Universe] to cause the most complex, refined literary form to coincide with the very way in which he Himself created all things in six days? Artistic form is in no sense opposed to an actual relation of facts, especially since the Author of the account is none less than the actual Creator of the facts which are described in that account.[139]

It is disturbing to see that Blocher admits that the author of Genesis 1 has given to the text a plain, straightforward meaning, which can nevertheless be discarded on the basis of a subjective appreciation of its artistic composition. How many literary devices do we need to find in a narrative before we may be sure that its straightforward meaning is disposable? Which refined literary forms are more decisive than others? How can such arguments be tested? Is it possible for any modern reader to scrutinize the mind of an ancient reader to ascertain if the propositions are sound? Who decides when we may ignore the plain meaning of a text and where we should stop reading figuratively the book of Genesis and start accepting its plain meaning again? Douglas F. Kelly points to the same false dilemma and warns us of the dangers of this approach:

> For, in the interests of this theory, they have introduced a potentially disastrous dichotomy between literary form and historical, chronological viability in interpreting biblical texts. It is naive to suppose that such a far-reaching hermeneutical dualism could be stopped at the end of the second chapter of Genesis, and would not be employed in other texts that run contrary to current naturalistic assumptions.[140]

John MacArthur raises a similar concern:

> The problem with the framework hypothesis is that it employs a destructive method of interpretation. If the plain meaning of Genesis 1 may be written off and the language treated as nothing more than a literary device, why not do the same with Genesis 3? Indeed, most theological liberals do insist that the talking serpent in chapter 3 signals a fable or a metaphor, and therefore they reject that passage as a literal and historical record of how humanity fell into sin. Where does metaphor ultimately end and history begin? After the flood? After the tower of Babel? And why there? Why not regard all the biblical miracles as literary devices? Why could not the resurrection itself be dismissed as a mere allegory?[141]

Marc Kay, who has examined the literary theory's philosophical foundations, judges that "contemporary interest in literary theory. . . is frequently mingled with, or characterised by a fundamental dependency upon, a postmodernist epistemology."[142] This recent trend, which obtains the meaning of a passage from its structure and shape, focuses on aesthetics and artistic stimulation. Literary theorists "reconfigure meaning of the biblical text through something other than the brute semantic information conveyed by the author's words themselves, the communicators of objective historical events."[143] Textual meaning will not arise from the text, which refers to actual historical events, but from the community of readers, who have their own artistic appreciation of the text. Meaning thus becomes relative rather than absolute. This post-modern epistemological approach downplays or even eliminates the importance of content, and considers questions of historicity as, for the most part, irrelevant.

In his second article, Kay's detailed examination of the literary devices that Genesis 1 is mooted to contain leads him to conclude that their presence does not rule out its being historical prose, to the contrary. The literary devices that the theory's proponents suggest as being included in Genesis 1 are either absent or, if present, do not entail non-historicity. Kay examines biblical narratives with devices such as intricate structure, alternation, rhythm, parallelism, chiasmus, repetition, number symbolism, and other literary patterns. He observes that parallelism actually occurs in prose, but the kind of parallelism that is characteristic of Hebrew poetry is absent in Genesis 1. As for repetition in this text, the following formulas are well-known: "And God said. . . And it was so. . . And God saw that it was good. . . And there was evening and there was morning." The Pentateuch and the rest of the Bible contain a great number of examples of parallelism, chiasmus, and repetition; and yet, these do not cast any doubt upon the temporal nature of these narratives. If structure, style, and literary complexity connote ahistoricity, then conservative literary theorists would have to reject *all* of the Bible's historical narratives. Following the classic historico-grammatical approach to the text, Kay reaffirms that the narrative sections of Scripture—including Genesis 1—are realistic. The words and sentences of the creation account really mean what they say, thus accurately describing real events that took place in a precise chronological order during a specific period of time. Kay warns us as follows:

> Patterns unaccompanied by supporting realities are vain parodies of themselves. Thus. . . an ascription of creative orderliness by a pattern, without the cosmos' earliest history first being orderly, is meaningless. This belief that the concern of Genesis' author is atemporal is one replete with irony. It is ironic because such a misunderstanding opens the door to nothing less than a full revisitation by a pagan worldview. As several authors have extensively indicated, the removal of real time or chronological history is a marker for paganism. It cannot be an outlook informed by Jewish concerns because a biblical, Hebraic mindset was deeply and inextricably attached to 'the march of time.' Indeed, God himself was 'in time', so the writer of Genesis could not but reflect this also.[144]

Other examples from well-known narrative sections in the books of Moses may be helpful. For example, the Flood history in Genesis 6–8 is written in a well-structured literary form. It does not mean that the seven days Noah waited in the ark, the 40 days of rain, the 150 days the waters prevailed, the 40 days before the opening of the window, and the two times seven days between the sending of the dove are all to be taken figuratively. We understand that the literary style serves the history that is narrated. We find this in the book of Genesis itself. The ten plagues of Egypt is another example that illustrates it well. The ten plagues are organized according to a pattern of 3 + 3 + 3 + 1. It does not mean that the ten plagues are not presented in a chronological order, or that their sequence reveals a figurative meaning as opposed to a literal meaning.

Ray adds the following texts, which contain literary devices that do not downplay their historicity at all: Exodus 2:1–10, Leviticus 5:6, Ruth 1:8–9; 2:21–22 and Deuteronomy 21:10–11 (passages which contain gender-matched parallelism); the Flood narrative of Genesis 7:19–24; 9:1–7, 18–29; the circumcision accounts of Genesis 17:10–14, 23–27; the record of the blasphemer's punishment in Leviticus 24:10–23; God's promise of a son to the elderly Abraham and Sarah in Genesis 18:1–16; the sacrifice of Isaac in Genesis 22:1–19; God's revelation at Sinai in Exodus 19–24 (passages which contain chiastic structure); the Noachian covenant of Genesis 9 in which "Be fruitful and multiply, and fill the earth" is repeated in verses 1 and 7; Leviticus 19 with its frequent consecutive "I am the Lord" or "I am the Lord your God," which exemplifies immediate repetition.

Thus, the literary style and the artistic beauty of the form serve the purpose of God's revelation. God beautifully reveals to us events that really took place in space and *in time*. The literary form is not opposed to a "naive" or realist reading of the sequential events recorded. It simply gives more strength to this sequence.

Thematic structure vs strictly chronological meaning

The framework proponents repeatedly affirm that the days of Genesis 1 are topical rather than strictly chronological. But why should we oppose "thematic structure" and "strictly chronological meaning"? The preceding remarks have shown that the existence of an organized topical structure in two triads is not so simple to prove, and that "topical" and "chronological" do not need to be opposed to each other. Some more comments are required here.

First, the grammar of Genesis 1 needs to be taken into consideration. The first verb is in the perfect tense (*bara*, "created"), followed by a series of *waw* consecutives linked to verbs in the imperfect tense (*wayomer Elohim*, "And God said," etc.). This is usually characteristic of a historical narration in the Hebrew grammar, as McCabe has pointed out:

> Thus, the use of the *waw* consecutive in the prologue to the historical narrative of Genesis, Genesis 1:1–2:3, is consistent with the narrative material found in the remainder of Genesis. If Moses did not intend the creation account to be taken sequentially, then why did he so frequently use a grammatical form that is regularly used for sequence?[145]

The other item that demonstrates that the creation account is not a poetic text is the absence of linear parallelisms, which is a key poetic device.[146] In this case, the narration is confirmed by the announcement of the creative act, the command, the report, the evaluation, the alternation "day and night," the numerical sequence, etc.

Secondly, it is clear that the historical narrative account presents *successive acts* of creation. Each of the days *is built upon* what has been created during the preceding days. "God works with discernible order. The creation account unfolds progressively with each creative act laying the foundation for the next."[147]

For example, the waters, which are created at the beginning of the first day (1:2), are separated on the second day by the creation of the expanse. This expanse later receives the lights on the fourth day. The waters under the expanse, which have been separated by the creation of the expanse on the second day, are gathered on the third day to make the dry ground appear. The vegetation is created on the second part of the third day on this dry ground and will serve for food to the animals and man created the following days. The sea animals of the fifth day are placed in the seas, which already exist since the third day. The birds of the fifth day and the land animals of the sixth day will live and reproduce on the ground, which appeared on the third day. As for man, the crown of the creation, he is placed on a habitable earth. He is given the mandate to rule over the different animals, and the fruit-bearing plants are presented as his food. All this has been created during the preceding days.

As for the first and fourth days, it has been shown earlier that their alleged "temporal recapitulation" has no solid basis and is contradicted by the text of the Bible itself. We have seen that the first day and the fourth day are not a recapitulation at all, but they reveal a precise temporal progression. This progression goes from the real separation of light and darkness on the first day to the established, good and complete separation of light and darkness on the fourth day, when governed by the lights in the expanse. W. Grudem says:

> Finally, the strongest argument against the framework view, and the reason why comparatively few evangelicals have adopted it, is that the whole of Genesis 1 strongly suggests not just a literary framework but a chronological sequence of events. When the narrative proceeds from the less complex aspects of creation (light and darkness, waters, sky, and dry land) to the more complex aspects (fish and birds, animals and man) we see a progressive build-up and an ordered sequence of events that are entirely understandable chronologically.[148]

Even though Godfrey holds that "the days of creation are figurative descriptions of the actions of God,"[149] he repeatedly detects a clear progression during the creation week and a well organized development in God's creative acts from day one to day six.

> God shows us that his purpose in creation is not some kind of static, unchanging reality. Just as time is built into creation from the beginning, so is development. God in his creation is already pointing us to a fulfillment or consummation of that creation. Theologians would say that God builds eschatology into creation at the beginning. God is already preparing us for the idea of a final completion of his work that is more developed than what is created at first. The end will be better than the beginning.[150]

> God's work on the second day closes with the familiar words, "And there was evening, and there was morning – the second day." Those words are so familiar we may miss the point: Moses is reminding us that the work of the first day carries over to the second day. On the second day we have not only the new work of separating the waters but also the continuation of the work of the first day, namely, the creation of the day.[151]

> The third day again not only records the creative acts of that day but also alludes to the creative events of the earlier days. The waters separated, the sky, and the day are also mentioned along with the dry land and the vegetation.[152]
>
> Why would Genesis 1 have an apparently chronological form? One partial answer is that a succession of days is presented in the text because each day of creation carries with it references to the creative accomplishments of the earlier days. Therefore each act of creation contains a reference to day because "day" was the first creative act. We can see this reiteration in the fourth day in reference to the elements created on earlier days: the day, the light, the sky, the earth (presumably including the seas and the dry land), and the vegetation (implied in seasons governed by the sun and moon). And when God saw that it was good, he was viewing not only the lights that he had created but also the accumulated works of all his previous activities.[153]
>
> On this fifth day the reiteration of the earlier aspects of creation are again mentioned or alluded to: the day (and implicitly the sun), the water, and the land (and implicitly the vegetation).[154]
>
> Genesis 1 presents creation as the progressive ordering of the earth to be a home for man in fellowship with God and to teach man how he is to bear God's image.[155]
>
> The days show the progressive way in which God solved the three problems of Genesis 1:2 to make the earth habitable for humankind.[156]

Godfrey even criticizes the framework view on this point:

> The framework's approach to the days of Genesis as figurative does not seem fully to explain the chronological and sequential character of the text.[157]

Thus, Genesis 1 does not present sequentially disconnected topics or "picture frames" but a magnificent and a masterly *historical progression.* It is not for nothing that this progression is given emphasis by the approving refrain "And God saw that it was good." This progression comes to a climax on the sixth day by a judgment over the whole of the creation (and not just over the work of the sixth day, as if this day were a picture equivalent to the five other pictures): "And God saw everything that he had made, and behold, it was very good" (1:31).

> Step by step in majestic grandeur God worked to transform the unformed earth into a world upon which man might dwell and which man might rule for God's glory. How noble and beautiful is this purpose, a purpose which is obscured and even obliterated when once we deny that the six days are to be taken in sequence.[158]

In summary, the progressive work of the Creator is well-ordered in the succession of time. It expresses that His purpose and design are filled with wisdom and find a glorious accomplishment at the end of the week of creation. The chronological sequence of the days of creation is entirely to His glory![159]

Meaning and purpose vs facts and history

Proponents of the figurative view have the tendency to propose many other false dilemmas in order to justify their views. It is a well known fact that the old liberal theologians and the higher criticism of the Bible have destroyed the faith of many people and past generations by postulating an antithesis between the theological meaning of the text and the brute facts of history. Even though most of the proponents of the figurative view believe that the God of the Bible created the heavens and the earth and that Genesis 1 and 2 are true, historical accounts of creation, and not a myth, it is alarming to see conservative theologians swallowing and teaching a false dichotomy between meaning and history that they claim to detect in the creation account of Genesis. Godfrey also says:

> Genesis is not written as a history book for uninformed, worldwide readers but is part of the covenant history written for a covenant people who already know their God.[160]

> The character of the revelation is not to tell us about creation in the abstract but about the appearance and meaning of creation for God's image bearer. Genesis 1 is not an encyclopedia of history or science but a covenant revelation of the character of the creation that God made for man.[161]

> [God] uses seven days to reveal the week that will be a fundamental part of the rhythm of human life. He is not showing us exactly the time he took to create but is revealing to us the way in which the seven-day week will order our lives as his people.[162]

> God's primary concern in both accounts [Gen. 1 and 2] is not to give us a specific chronology of God's acts but to show us God's meaning and purpose for humanity in creation.[163]

> All of our considerations of the Bible's teaching on days and time should lead us to the conclusion that the days and week of Genesis 1 are presented to us as a real week of twenty-four-hour days. These days and week, however, do not describe God's actions in themselves but present God's creative purpose in a way that is a model for us.[164]

> So Genesis 1 as a whole focuses not so much on how God made the world for man but on the meaning, purpose, and order of that creation for man.[165]

After all his careful analysis of the progressive development of God's creative acts, it is very perplexing and disappointing to see that Godfrey comes to this completely illogical conclusion. Why does he so bluntly contradict himself? He says that "God builds into creation at the beginning,. . . preparing us for the idea of a final completion." Is it just an *idea* that God has revealed to us, or is it a true historical fact? Godfrey clearly speaks of "God's work on the second day," "the creation of the day," "creative events," "creative acts of the third day," "creative accomplishments of the earlier days," "accumulated works of all his previous activities," "the progressive ordering of the earth," etc. Suddenly, he turns around and says that Genesis 1 is *not* so much about God's actions in themselves *but* about His purpose for us. It is *not* about a specific chronology of God's acts *but* about God's meaning and purpose for humanity. It is *not* about the time He took to create *but* about the way He wants us to live, etc. Where do these oppositions come from? Godfrey wrongly deduces them from the fact that God uses the pattern of a week in His work of creation that was meant to teach us moral lessons. Jim Witteveen makes these useful observations:

> If Genesis 1 is "covenantal" in its character, does that necessarily mean that it is not a history of the world? Of course, Godfrey does use the phrases "world history text" and "encyclopedia of history or science," seeming to assert that those who argue for the "six consecutive real days that actually happened in history view" consider the first chapter of the Bible to be a scientific treatise of some sort. This kind of language is not at all helpful, and it mischaracterizes those who believe in six actual historical days.[166]

> Did God use a recognizable pattern in His work of creation? Yes, He did, and that pattern was meant to teach us many very important things. But to say that His work is recorded in a pattern that is meant to teach, and that the creation account is "covenantal" is not to exclude the fact that what is recorded is a true and accurate account of actual events. Our God is the God of history, not merely the God of ideas. Here is the fatal flaw in Godfrey's examination of Genesis 1.[167]

Proponents of the figurative views tend to say that they are sure that they know what the primary purpose of God was when He wrote Genesis. It usually indicates that they cannot accept the literal interpretation of the text. God wrote what He wrote for our information. We can derive beautiful meaning from this, see patterns and implications, be assured of His care for us and be led to praise Him. But we must not think that we know the mind of God better than He does Himself or place words in His mouth that He does not say Himself.

From Scripture in general and from Genesis 1 in particular, there is no reason to oppose two things that are harmoniously and closely connected. Godfrey's assertions create a conflict where there is none. "Six days you shall labor, and do all your work, but the seventh day is a Sabbath to the Lord your God. On it you shall not do any work" (Ex. 20:9–10). This is how we should live. Then follows the historical and chronological fact that gives the solid foundation to how we should live: "For in six days the Lord made heaven and earth, the sea, and all that is in them, and rested on the seventh day" (Ex. 20:11). According to the Bible itself, the days of creation *are* primarily about God's creative acts and about the time it took God to create the world. God's mighty acts must first be proclaimed, then follow the privileges given to us, coupled with the moral obligations for us.

Yes, God gives a history book that we must make known to the world, *and* this book is more particularly relevant for His covenant people. Yes, Genesis 1 is about God's creation, *and consequently* these creative acts have purpose and meaning for God's image bearers. Yes, God is showing us the time He took to create with a specific chronology, *and consequently* the fact that He took six days and rested on the seventh is the foundation ordering our lives and weeks as His people. The days and week of Genesis 1 describe God's actions, *and consequently* they present God's creative purpose in a way that is a model for us. Genesis as a whole focuses on how God made the world for man, *and consequently* this work of creation gives meaning, purpose and order of that creation for man. When we oppose these "good friends," the message of Genesis becomes only a moral message, based on the "revealed idea" but not on the *revealed fact* that God created in six days.

4

The Unending Seventh Day

We have seen in a preceding chapter that the so-called unending seventh day is an important argument in favour of the figurative view. We concluded that the absence of the "evening-morning" formula is fully in harmony with the literal view. We need, however, to go a step further. What the figurative proponents write regarding the so-called unending seventh day is very problematic and disconcerting.

On the one hand, they assert the clear and simple meaning of the days of the creation week, understood as a normal seven-day week. "At this point we agree with the 24-hour theorists that at the literal level, Genesis 1 speaks of seven ordinary days."[168] Of course, they insist that the *total* picture of the divine workweek be taken figuratively. But when the Bible's teaching on days and time is carefully considered, "the days and week of Genesis 1 are presented to us as a real week of twenty-four-hour days."[169] Clearly, at the literal level, the absence of "evening and morning" does not prevent them from understanding that the week ends with a seventh day of normal length, similar in this regard to all the other days of the week. This is the only way that the creation week can be considered "a stereotype from the biblical writer's cultural milieu"[170] and "a model timetable for us to follow."[171]

On the other hand, the figurative proponents somewhere change their mind, insisting that the seventh day of Genesis 1 is, after all, an unending period of time. Here are the opinions of Mark Ross, the OPC Committee to Study the Framework Hypothesis, and Irons and Kline, respectively:

> "God's Sabbath is most assuredly not a twenty-four hour day. Beginning His rest on the seventh, that day had no end. There was no 'evening and morning' for that day."[172]

> Indeed, the day that ends the creation week is clearly not a literal 24-hour day, even though it also is referred to by the name "day." It has neither evening nor morning. It is eternal. It is God's heavenly rest into which Adam is invited but fails to enter through disobedience."[173]

> The creation week *concludes* with an upper-register day of rest for God. . . This seventh day is not an earthly day of rest for man, but the heavenly rest of God Himself. Because it is synonymous with God's heavenly enthronement, the seventh day argues for the upper-register nature of the creation week, and as an eternal day, it argues for the nonliteral nature of the creation days. . . In fact, the absence of the "evening-morning" formula at the conclusion of the seventh day flags this day as unique in that it has no end. Now if the seventh day was unending and eternal, it certainly cannot be an ordinary, lower-register day. But if the seventh day is an upper-register day, the entire week of which it is an integral part must be an upper-register "week" as well.[174]

No matter how one looks at the argument, this position manifestly appears to be internally self-contradictory. How is it possible, in the first place, to say that the absence of an evening and a morning forces us to understand the seventh day as being unending, while at the literal level no such obligation is required? After all, no "abnormal" week ending with a seventh unending day was ever possible for Moses to observe in his cultural milieu nor will ever be a possible model timetable for us to follow week after week. Even literary theorists understand that Genesis 1, in spite of the absence of an evening and a morning at the end of the seventh day, still speaks of seven days of ordinary length—including the seventh—and not six days of ordinary length plus a seventh unending day.

Moreover, how is it possible to say that the seven-day week is a figurative framework, but that the seventh day, after all, is real historical? The so-called unending nature of the seventh day does not make it figurative; it simply makes it eternal, but still very real. No matter how one views the seventh day—as belonging to a heavenly reality in the "upper register" or as belonging to an earthly reality in the "lower register"—the question remains the same. If the absence of an evening and a morning in the description of the seventh day points to a true historical unending period of time, then the *very presence* of an evening and a morning in the description of each of the previous six days should, conversely, point to six true historical periods of time—six true historical days. It is not possible to have it both ways. The fact that there is no evening and morning at the end of the seventh day—according to the framework proponents—necessarily means it is an unending, real day; but the fact that there is an evening and a morning after each of the previous days would have absolutely no bearing on the real, factual nature and length of these days. The evening-morning formula would be simply a detail in the creation-week picture, a refrain functioning as part of the formularized framework of the account; but the absence of the formula would be decisive for understanding the unending nature of the seventh day. This reasoning is simply inconsistent, based on a fallacious logic.

Irons and Kline sense the problem when they speak of an "upper-register week." They do not venture to explain what an "upper-register week" could consist of (in terms of length, sequence, and synchronization with the "lower-register level"). But no matter to which "register" the week of creation belongs, the following question remains: Are these two registers real or not? Is the week part of a real historical progression, or is it figurative of something else? In other words, is the figurative view of the week still figurative? More specifically, does the framework view still consider the creation week as only a literary framework to describe earthly creative events? Remember, according to Irons and Kline themselves, quoted at the beginning of this study, the framework interpretation is defined as follows:

> It is that interpretation of Genesis 1:1–2:3 which regards the seven-day scheme as a figurative framework. While the six days of creation are presented as normal solar days, according to the framework interpretation the total picture of God's completing His creative work in a week of days is not to be taken literally. Instead it functions as a literary structure in which the creative works of God have been narrated in a topical order. The days are like picture frames.[175]

But now, contradicting themselves, they claim that the week is much more than a literary framework or picture frames intended to classify in a topical order the earthly creative events. The entire week is an upper-register week in which God lives and of which the real seventh unending day is an integral part. Here, we may seize the opportunity to pause for a moment and honestly ask this question: Is their view still a "framework" view? Or are the days being defined in every possible imaginative ways, provided they are *not* literal earthly days?

The figurative arguments are so difficult to follow that the figurative proponents themselves often contradict each other. For Irons and Kline, the seventh day "is not an earthly day of rest for man, but the heavenly rest of God Himself." But for the OPC Committee to Study the Framework Hypothesis, "It is God's heavenly rest into which Adam is invited but fails to enter through disobedience." Irons and Kline specify that "if the seventh day was unending and eternal, it certainly cannot be an ordinary, lower-register day." A confusion is made between an ordinary day and a lower-register reality. An unending reality does not necessarily belong to heaven; it may also belong to earthly history. For example, when God created the lights on the fourth day, the unending reality of the seasons and years began (until it stops when Christ returns). When someone is miraculously born of the Holy Spirit, the unending reality of eternal life begins in this person's life here on earth (and will never stop).

For this reason, Ross says, "This is God's Sabbath rest, in which he now lives," a Sabbath that "spans the whole of earth history from the end of the sixth day, however that is understood, to its consummation in Christ."[176] Contrary to Irons and Kline, the Sabbath, for him, apparently belongs both to the heavenly realm and to the earthly history. As for Godfrey, the creation days "are for us as a model for our working, not as a time schedule that God followed."[177] Contrary to Kline's concept of a Sabbath related exclusively to an upper-register week in which God lives and acts, and contrary to Ross's opinion to the effect that the Sabbath belongs both to God's heavenly life and to earthly history, for Godfrey, "the days are actual for us but figurative for God. They are not a timetable of God's actions but are a model timetable for us to follow."[178] Everyone seems to find a different, contradictory meaning, provided the meaning is *not* literal historical days. This phenomenon is the sort of post-modern relativist artistic appreciation of the text that was described in the preceding chapter. Each interpreter brings a particular meaning to the text, based on one's own sensitivity to its form and structure, instead of simply accepting the straightforward meaning of the text.

Which interpreter is correct and how can we know? How can a sincere ordinary believer navigate through such an indecipherable maze of contradictory concepts, and find a way out? Obviously, the different figurative views discussing the meaning of the seventh day pile up insurmountable problems that are absent from the literal interpretation. The fourth commandment uses the word "day" for six days you shall labor, for the days of creation, for the Sabbath, and for the seventh day, always assuming that the reader understands these to be regular days, with an evening and a morning. Those who first heard these words did not interrupt Moses and say, "Which days do you mean? Literal? Figurative? Upper register? Model timetable?"

In conclusion, according to the simple meaning of the days in Exodus 20:8–11 and the plain, straightforward meaning of Genesis 1:1–2:3, there is no reason to understand the seventh day of the creation week as anything other than a day of normal length. As Louis Berkhof says, "The sabbath of the creation week was a day equal in length to the other days. God not only rested on that day, but He also blessed and hallowed it, setting it aside as a day of rest for man, Ex. 20:11. This would hardly apply to the whole period from the time of creation up to the present day."[179] If the Sabbath set aside for rest certainly was a literal day, then it reinforces the conclusion that the other days were of the same kind.

5

"Background"

Some framework proponents have proposed that the *intent* of the author of Genesis was not to explain to us the chronology of the creative acts of God but to prepare the people of Israel to enter into Canaan and live in covenant relationship with their Lord. According to this view, the book of Genesis is only a preamble to the covenant concluded at Mount Sinai and to the entrance of God's people into the promised land.[180] Here is the opinion of Godfrey and Futato, respectively:

> Indeed one way to see the whole Book of Genesis is as an historical introduction to God's covenant made with his people at Sinai. . . The Book of Genesis provides the historical background to that covenanting at Sinai. . . The origins or roots of the people who met with God at Sinai are the central concern of the Book of Genesis.[181]

> The ubiquitous threat of Baalism provides the theological context in which Genesis 1–2 is to be read. . . Genesis 1–2 proclaims that YHWH, the God of Israel, is the Lord of the rain, the resultant vegetation, and life. This central aspect of the message of Genesis 1–2 is embedded in the structure of the accounts. Why the two-fold focus on vegeta-

> tion and the people that live on that vegetation? Why even bring into consideration the lack of vegetation owing to a lack of rain? Is this simply geographical decoration? No, for the book of Genesis serves as the prologue to the history of Israel. Genesis makes the point that the God of the nation of Israel is the God of Abraham, Isaac, and Jacob (Genesis 12–50), and that the God of Abraham, Isaac, and Jacob is the Creator of the heavens and the earth (Genesis 1–11). The God of Israel is the Creator. From the beginning, the God of Israel, not Baal, has been the provider of the rain that is the prerequisite for life. *YHWH God of Israel has been the Lord of the rain from the beginning!*[182]

For this reason, Moses was supposedly not really interested in the age of the earth or by the chronological details of the creative acts. His main concern was to prepare Israel to face the pagan idolatry that reigned in Canaan. According to this view, the purpose of the first chapters of Genesis is simply to remind them that God is the Creator of everything and the Lord of rain, vegetation, and life, and that the world belongs to Him.

Many things may be said about the presumed intent of an author. It is one thing to claim knowing the intent of the author; it is another thing proving it, especially when we claim that the author's intent could *not* have been this or that. Where is the proof, in the first place, that the background of Genesis 1 is the preparation for the entrance of Israel into Canaan and the conflict between their faith and the false pagan gods of Canaan? What gives us the assurance that the purpose of Genesis 1 is to be a preamble to the Sinaitic covenant? The only way we can know the intent of the author is to read *what he says*. The problem is that we do not find any reference to the pagan gods of Canaan or to the Sinaitic covenant or to the entrance into the promised land in Genesis 1–2. Furthermore, this approach raises the Sinaitic covenant above the covenants made with Adam, Noah, and the patriarchs, while these covenants are belittled as "preliminary" covenants.

Besides, we could equally affirm that the background of Genesis is *Egyptian*, since Egypt is where Moses and Israel came from.[183] There the sun and the stars were worshipped. In that context, Moses could have considered the chronological order of the creation of the sun after the light something important to affirm.

As for the critical approach to the Bible, Hermann Gunkel (1862–1932) and those who followed his critical methodology of form criticism postulated that the background of Genesis is *Babylonian*. Gunkel, an outstanding representative of the "History of Religions School," compared the creation account of the Bible with Babylonian mythology, with a view to discovering the origin and development of the myth and of biblical religion. The purpose was to try to find out a presumed earlier history of the narrative. He wrongly concluded that the "legends" of Genesis have borrowed several ideas from those pagan myths, while at the same time rejecting several of their polytheist views (a legend being the product of the whole people, the expression of the people's mind).

According to liberal, critical scholars, Genesis 1 is considered as a myth similar to other ancient cosmogonies, whose purpose was to explain the present world, an explanation lacking historical credibility. Having discovered a number of parallels between the biblical creation account and a Babylonian creation epic, the *Enuma Elish*, Gunkel and many other liberal scholars argued that ancient Babylonian traditions shaped the Hebrew people's perceptions of God's creative activity at the beginning of time. They forgot that there is at least another possibility, namely, that the Babylonian story is a corrupted version of the true historical events recorded in Genesis. They also rejected the possibility that the story of creation was revealed without error directly to Moses or to one of the earlier patriarchs who passed it on to Moses under the guidance of the Holy Spirit. Surprisingly, similar critical views about a supposed dependence of the biblical creation narrative upon Babylonian mythology are being repeated today by so-called "conservative" Reformed and Evangelical theologians. Their wrong teaching is more and more influencing the church's understanding of Genesis 1.

The attacks—whether virulent or insidious, frontal or subtle—against the veracity of the biblical creation account come from every possible angle. The reason is that the first three chapters of Genesis, recording the creation of the world, the fall into sin, and the promise of redemption, are foundational to all the other biblical doctrines and to our Christian faith and life—and the enemy knows it.

Genesis 1 is admittedly an indirect polemic against idolatry of every time, but is that its sole, or even its main, concern?[184] In fact, the text does not mention any opposition whatsoever to any ancient idolatrous practices, as opposed to the overt polemic found in several passages of the book of Isaiah, for instance, which mock the vain idols of Israel's enemies. In that case, it is easy to prove the polemic nature of these prophetic texts, since they explicitly refer to idols and their vanity. But in Genesis 1 there is no such mention of idols. It is difficult to find allusions to idolatry even in the rest of the book of Genesis (there is a brief mention of *teraphim* in Genesis 31). The endeavour to find out clues or hints of polemic against idolatry "between the lines" or "behind" the text of Genesis 1 then becomes risky and subjective. A pastor using this method of "eisegesis" will tend to preach "above" the text and will feel free to incorporate his own opinions in his sermons, instead of faithfully preaching what the Word of God really says.

Even if we admit that the background of Genesis 1 is the entrance into Canaan, there is no proof that the chronological and sequential order of the days of creation was not important for Moses and especially for the divine Author. Why did Moses make such effort to write in such a refined literary form a general truth that he could have preached to the Israelites in one or two sentences? "The Lord is the only true God and the idols must be rejected. The Lord is the Creator of heaven and earth, the Lord of rain, and all that

He created is good." Something similar would have been enough.

Genesis 1–2 reveals to us much more than this general truth. For example, Christ sees in this text the foundation of marriage and the reason for rejecting divorce (Matt. 19:5–6). Paul discovers in Genesis 2 principles for the relations between man and woman. In 1 Corinthians 11:8 and 1 Timothy 2:13 the chronological detail of the creation of the man before the woman is the basis of his argument. This detail is very important for him and for the Holy Spirit. It is the foundation of the order of the marital relations as well as of the relations between men and women in the church.

Did Moses and Israel need to know this chronological detail? Yes, as much as Noah, Abraham, and the Christians of the twenty-first century do, since all Scripture is breathed out by God and profitable for teaching, for reproof, for correction, and for training in righteousness (2 Tim. 3:16). Genesis was not written only for those who were going to enter into Canaan. Moreover, in Israel it was not only the fight against idols that was important. The relationship with God, marital and family life, work and rest, etc., were also important, even primordial. It is still true for the Church today, which needs the light of the totality of the Word of God.

What about the six literal days of the creation followed by the day of rest, blessed and sanctified by the Lord? Did Israel need to know this chronological detail in order to live in a covenant relationship with God in the promised land? Exodus 20:8–11 shows this to be the case. The Word of God tells us here how the people of Israel should have a rhythm to their weekly life in their new life in Canaan. The weekly rhythm of work and worship is not something of little importance in the life of the covenant people. The observance of the Sabbath is even called a *sign* of the covenant (Ex. 31:16–17). The *motivation* for this commandment is precisely the model that God gave them: "Six days you shall labor, and do all your work, but the seventh day is a Sabbath to the Lord your God. On it you shall not do any work. . . For in six days the Lord made heaven and earth, the sea, and all that is in them, and rested the seventh day. Therefore the Lord blessed the Sabbath day and made it holy" (Ex. 20:9–11).

We are on solid ground here to know not only the intent of the human author but especially the intent of the Lord Himself, when He created the world in six days and rested the seventh. For God could easily have created everything instantaneously. Why did He create in six days followed by a seventh day? Because it is a cycle He imposed on man for his well-being, especially for the well-being of His covenant people, and for God's glory. It is a cycle that God imposed on Himself when He created, because He loved His creation. He made all His creative work in six days and rested on the seventh day so that man could imitate his Creator and be blessed by Him.

6

The Analogy Of Faith

The framework proponents assert that they subscribe to the Reformed hermeneutical principle whereby the Bible interprets itself. They say they apply this principle to the way they treat Genesis 1 and 2. This principle is excellent, and we subscribe to it wholeheartedly. The question is whether the framework interpretation really does respect this principle.

We have seen that there is no problem with considering the days of Genesis 1 as real, consecutive days of normal length, when Genesis 1 is compared with Genesis 2. Besides, it is wise and helpful to use a clear text (Gen. 1) in order to interpret a less clear text (Gen. 2:5). To do the opposite, as is done by the framework theory, seems risky. Many have also shown that there is not one allusion in the first chapters of Genesis themselves suggesting that the days are figurative days. Therefore, we must look for clues outside of Genesis 1 and 2.

The book of Genesis – its genre, outline and content

Let us first look at the rest of the book of Genesis. The unity of the book – both of its content and of its form – may certainly help us come to a better understanding of the first two chapters of the book and may help us figure out how these chapters are related to the whole. For instance, what is the literary genre of the book of Genesis? Since this book is not poetic, semi-poetic or figurative, but fundamentally historical, it should be expected that the beginning of the book be the same literary genre as the rest of the book (as opposed to the book of Revelation, for instance, with its highly symbolic nature; its numbers—three, four, seven, one thousand, etc.—must be understood in the context of the literary genre of this book).[185]

It has also been shown that the repetitive use of the Hebrew word *toledoth* (meaning "generations," "posterities," "history," or "outcome") is a key to understanding the structure of Genesis and the development of thought within the book. This word is repeated ten times in the book of Genesis (2:4; 5:1; 6:9; 10:1; 11:10; 11:27; 25:12; 25:19; 36:1; 37:2). It gives an outline that specifically emphasizes the historical nature of the book and the particular posterities through which God accomplished His redemptive work after the fall. Thus the first section (1:1–2:3), presenting the creation of the heavens and the earth, is a historical introduction to the rest of the book, followed by the first *toledoth* telling what has come out of the heavens and the earth (2:4–4:26), followed by the second *toledoth* telling what has come out of Adam, meaning the line from him to Noah (5:1–6:8), whose *toledoth* will be the next (6:9–9:25), etc.

God's creative activities "in the beginning" is followed by a more detailed history, with people, plots, genealogies, and chronological information about the main characters and events. The whole book of Genesis is historical, and the temporal reference points are important to locate both the Flood narrative and the different stages of the lives of the patriarchs. There is no reason to see the days of Genesis 1 as chronologically meaningless or disconnected from the rest of the historical progression narrated in the book. The flashbacks observed between *toledoth* do not change anything to the accuracy of each chronological information within each *toledoth*. This also applies to the creation days, which are specifically punctuated by evenings and mornings and clearly qualified by a numerical order. The whole book of Genesis does not suggest in any way the figurative interpretation of the days of creation; on the contrary, it fully supports a literal interpretation.

Day, evening, and morning in the Pentateuch

Another question needs to be addressed: In which sense does the rest of the book of Genesis use the words "day," "evening and morning," and "first, second, third. . ."? In his historical books, does Moses use the word "day" in a figurative way elsewhere? If so, in which context and what indications does he give to make us understand that it is figurative? It would be very helpful if the framework interpretation gave us some examples. It has been shown that in the Pentateuch the word "day," when associated with consecutive ordinal numbers (first, second, third, etc.), *always* has a literal sequential meaning (there are more than 110 occurrences; we have checked all of them, and not one of them has a figurative meaning). Why would Genesis 1 be the exception?[186]

As for the refrain "evening and morning," Peter Wallace wrongly concludes that "the usage of the terms 'evening' and 'morning' does not particularly lend itself to an ordinary day interpretation."[187] He bases his conclusion on the fact that the phrase does not refer to the whole day in any of the instances he found in the Old Testament. He wrongly presumes that the literal interpretation necessitates that the period described by "evening and morning" be a whole day. Wallace proposes instead the "analogical" interpretation of the days of creation—another non-literal view difficult to understand. He even says, "Never is the language of morning and evening (or evening and morning) used to refer to a literal 24-hour day." This affirmation is simply misleading and confuses the issue. It is fair to concede that "evening and morning" in Genesis 1 does not refer to the whole day. Actually, we would not expect anything else, since God creates something during day-time, followed by an evening and a morning referring to night-time, followed by the numbering of the completed day (*n*th day), followed by another creative activity the next day. "There was evening and there was morning" simply refers to the passage from the evening to the morning, not to the whole day.

Wallace examines the seventeen places in Scripture outside of Genesis 1 where the word "evening" (*erev*) precedes "morning" (*boqer*). This includes seven passages in the Pentateuch (Ex. 16:8; 16:13; 27:21; Lev. 24:3; Nb. 9:15, 21; 28:8; Deut. 16:4). He also examines the nineteen references where "morning" (*boqer*) precedes "evening" (*erev*), including six passages in the Pentateuch (Gen. 49:27; Ex. 18:13, 14; 29:39; Nb. 28:4; Deut. 28:67). The fact is that Wallace cannot find any occurrences of the words "evening" and "morning" that point to something else than *literal* evenings and mornings, except in Daniel 8:14 where they are apparently figurative ("the 2,300 days are indeed ordinary days—but they represent a different period of time"). Wallace has discovered from his study that "the language of 'evening and morning' is generally used to describe the period from the cessation of labor before sunset until the renewal of labor after sunrise." This is exactly what the refrain is all about in Genesis 1, according to the literal interpretation. God creates during day-time hours, not during night-time hours. What then is the problem with the interpretation of the days as literal if the evenings and the mornings are literal?

Exodus 20:8–11

If the Bible interprets itself, then it would be useful to find a passage somewhere else in the Bible that says or suggests that these days are figurative. That is not the case. For example, we do not read anywhere such a statement: "Six days you shall labor and do all your work, but on the seventh day you shall not do any work. For the Lord revealed his creative acts in a figure or a pattern of six days, and he revealed his rest in a figure of a seventh day." Many authors have shown as well that the whole New Testament presupposes the historical and chronological truthfulness of the events mentioned in the first two chapters of Genesis.[188]

On the other hand, the framework proponents have a hard time explaining the text of Exodus 20:8–11 in an accessible and intelligible way, without performing all kinds of semantic or theological gymnastics. It is not necessary to criticize in detail the eccentric explanations that some framework proponents have given to this text. Others have already done that sufficiently.[189] Still, this text must be taken into consideration if one wants to let the Bible interpret itself. When we read Exodus 20:8–11 from every possible angle, we cannot see in it anything but a literal chronological and sequential interpretation of the days of creation.

The fourth commandment contains two main parts. The first part is the commandment itself: "Six days you shall labor, and do all your work, but the seventh day is a Sabbath to the Lord your God. . ." The second part is the reason for this commandment: "For in six days the Lord made heaven and earth, the sea, and all that is in them, and rested on the seventh day." What God's covenant people is required to do is based on what the Lord did in the beginning.

Suppose we were now to replace "days" with "thematic pictures" or "heavenly days" in the reason given: "For in six thematic pictures (or heavenly days) the Lord made heaven and earth. . ." It should then be possible to replace the same word "days" with "thematic pictures" or "heavenly days" in the commandment itself: "Six thematic pictures (or heavenly days) you shall labor." It would make no sense. Otherwise, nothing in the Bible could be understood anymore. Any attempt made to understand the Bible would be doomed to despair. Ultimately, the ground for the fourth commandment would disappear altogether, the historical reason for this commandment becoming totally incomprehensible.

> This passage [Exodus 20:8–11] provides a crucial problem for the framework theory. The non-literal approach argues that the six days are not to be taken literally but are merely a framework in terms of which the events are reported. Why is this framework used? Sometimes this is represented as another anthropomorphism. God's creative activity is described in terms of a human work-week. However the fourth commandment says the precise reverse. God's activity is not described in terms of man's. Rather, man's work-week is shaped by God's activity.
>
> What can we infer about the narrative in Genesis 1 from this reference? At the very least there has to be some sort of divine activity which man can imitate. Further than that, it has to be an activity that is adequately represented by a pattern of six days of work and one of rest. Here the framework theory is shown to be untenable. For it alleges that the seven days of Genesis 1 are only a framework to describe events. God's activity did not have that form. How then could man imitate God's activity in the weekly cycle if God's activity was not originally as described in Genesis 1?[190]

Godfrey says that "Genesis 1 presents God's days of creation as a pattern for man with six days for work and one day for rest. The days of Genesis are not primarily about how God created."[191] Except that, in his previous discussion on Exodus 20, his explanation of the fourth commandment was extremely brief. He did not explain how it is possible to bluntly contradict this text of Scripture, which clearly says that the days of creation *are primarily* about how God created: "For in six days the Lord made heaven and earth, the sea, and all that is in them, and rested on the seventh day."

Some proponents of the figurative view affirm that God did not really rest on the seventh day because He was not really tired. He only presented Himself as resting in order to teach us to rest. Then perhaps God only presented Himself as working six days to teach us to work six days. The days of Genesis should be taken as a mere teaching device exhorting us to work six days and rest on the seventh. "He does not need rest, but we do. He is accommodating his revelation of his creating work to us and our needs. He speaks of himself in a way that serves as a model for us."[192] But if God says He rested, who are we to contradict His Word? The question is not whether God really rested, but what His rest consisted of. The simple answer is that God's rest consisted of ceasing from His creative works but not from His work in providence. Genesis 2:3 says, "So God blessed the seventh day and made it holy, because on it God rested from all his work that he had done *in creation*."

The framework proponents are desperately trying to tell us that God, in order to reveal His work of creation, used a human reality, the week of seven days. God would use the seven-day human week as a model in order to show us the harmonious order of His creation and to develop a theology of the Sabbath. And yet, Exodus 20:8–11 tells us precisely the *reverse*: it is the man who must imitate God and take Him as model. It is our Creator who presents Himself as an example, and it is the man who must "remember" the Sabbath and the days of creation in order to imitate the Lord during the whole week.

It would then be unreasonable to take the word "day" literally in one part of the commandment and figuratively in the other part. Sound exegesis requires that the word "day" be taken in the same sense in both instances. It would be impossible for man to imitate God's activity in a cycle of one week if this activity of God in the beginning was not displayed in the "earthly time" and in a literal week of creation as described in Genesis 1.[193] "Exodus 20:8–11 is significant in that it gives us a clear answer to the debated question about whether the 'days' of Genesis are to be taken literally. The commandment loses completely its cogency if they are not taken literally."[194]

The light in other Scripture passages

Some interesting texts of the Bible speak about the *light* in a way that helps to understand the relationship between the first day and the fourth day of the creation week. For example, in Ecclesiastes 12:2, the sun is distinguished from the light. As well, the moon and stars are similarly distinguished, a clear reflection on the difference between creation days one and four: ". . .before the sun and the light and the moon and the stars are darkened. . ." In Job 38:19–20, the light and the darkness dwell in an inaccessible and mysterious place that Job cannot reach or understand. "Where is the way to the dwelling of light, and where is the place of darkness, that you may take it to its territory and that you may discern the paths to its home?" The light is totally independent from the sun. There is also Psalm 104:1–2: "You are clothed with splendor and majesty, covering yourself with light as with a garment, stretching out the heavens like a tent."

Paul says that the work of regeneration in the heart of the sinner comes from the (re)creative Word of God. "For God, who said, 'Let light shine out of darkness,' has shone in our hearts to give the light of the knowledge of the glory of God in the face of Jesus Christ" (2 Cor. 4:6). For Paul, the sentence "Let light shine out of darkness" is the precise content of the creative word of God. The remarkable thing is that the distinction between the light and the darkness is made *without any mention of the sun*. The proclamation of the Word of the Gospel produces the light in the hearts of the elect in an immediate way, exactly the same way as the first Word of God produced the light in the world in an immediate way. This light of the Gospel produced in our hearts does not need any intermediary—any support or mediator (like a priest or sacraments, for example)—any more than the light produced by the creative Word needed the help of the sun to shine in the darkness. The Word alone is sufficient, as the Holy Spirit secretly works in us to open our hearts to this Word. It produces *a light complete in itself*. The re-creative Word of God is powerful to initiate and work regeneration in the darkened heart of the sinners, exactly the same way as His creative Word was powerful to produce the light, the first work of creation. Thus, the apostle Paul indirectly confirms that originally the light was independent from the sun.

We may also quote Revelation 21:23, where it says that in the new Jerusalem there will be "no need of sun or moon to shine on it," and 22:5, which says, "They will need no light of lamp or sun, for the Lord God will be their light." The new creation will be filled with a wonderful light. The sun and the moon were not there at the beginning, and they will not be there at the end. In fact, they are there only temporarily.[195]

Godfrey says that "elsewhere the Bible always links the light to the lights."[196] He quotes five passages from Scripture to support his claim but does not discuss Ecclesiastes 12:2, Job 38:19–20, Psalm 104:1–2, or 2 Corinthians 4:6. He first refers to Revelation 21:23 and 22:5. These texts necessarily link the light to the sun and the moon because John is giving us a glorious hope in the context of the present reality of our sufferings. John's purpose was not to explain the situation that prevailed during the first three days of creation.

The same may be said of the prophetic text of Isaiah 60:19–20. These statements about the new heaven and earth do not imply that in the old heaven and earth light came only from the lights. They only compare the difference between what exists now and the future glory in the new creation. As for Zechariah 14:6–7, it is not correct to say that this text links the light to the lights, since there is no mention of the sun or the moon. Interestingly, Zechariah only speaks of the light, the day, and the night, before the new glorious light will appear at the end of history. Finally, concerning Psalm 74:16–17, Godfrey sees things that are not in the text when he says that "the psalmist assumes that the sun rules the day and that God's creation of the day is through the sun." The sun rules the day since the fourth day of creation, but the psalmist does not say anything about God's creation of the day. He simply says that "yours is the day, yours also the night" – a present reality.

In conclusion, according to the analogy of faith, the rest of Scripture does not support the framework theory at all. On the contrary, it supports the literal meaning.

7

Other Problems

The age of the earth when Adam was created

As for the present age of the earth, many want to convince us that it is an independent subject from the creation/evolution debate. The evolutionists, however, know very well that if we could confirm that the earth is young, their theory would fall down like a house of cards. In the present Christian world, which is not very interested in biblical chronology, we should be suspicious of declarations like this: "The Bible certainly does not have anything to say about the age of the earth." This subject extends beyond Genesis 1 and would need a separate study (the genealogies of Genesis 5 and 11, the Flood narrative, the biblical chronology, etc.).

The only question raised here is this one: What was the age of the earth when Adam and Eve were created? According to the literal meaning of Genesis 1, the earth was only *six days old*. Our first parents were placed into a very young earth! In fact, there was no reason for God to wait any longer before giving to the earth the stewards of His creation, who were destined to govern and fill the earth. We might even say: It was *the normal providential plan* of God for the earth that man created in His image be placed on it as vice-regent right from the beginning. The domain of the earth could not justify its reason to exist in God's plan without its king. How is it possible to say that man is theologically the climax of the creation, but that historically he appears a few seconds before midnight on the clock of the universe?[197]

This may seem absurd to the eyes of modern secular scientific theories, and many Christians, under this strong pressure, may be embarrassed by the literal meaning of Genesis. The Gap Theory and the Day-Age Theory have tried to come to the rescue, but they have been strongly criticized both from a biblical perspective and from a scientific "concordance" perspective. The framework theory comes to the rescue and seems very convenient, since it simply avoids the confrontation with secular scientific theories on two aspects. Genesis 1 supposedly does not say anything about the *length* of the creative work, nor about the *sequence* of the creative acts. That is a real "advantage" compared with the Gap Theory and the Day-Age Theory. The age of the earth when Adam was created would be unknown to us because it would not have been revealed. Consequently this age could be very long, as modern "science" says.

We seem to forget what Christ himself said when he talked about marriage and divorce: "Have you not read that he who created them *from the beginning* made them male and female. . .?" (Matt. 19:4). In the same context, Mark 10:6 says more precisely, "But *from the beginning of creation*, God made them male and female." How can we maintain that the earth was old when God created the man and the woman? "From the beginning" does not simply mean the beginning of humanity but the beginning of creation. It is clear that the first words of Genesis 1:1 are quoted here. This presupposes a close chronological connection between the creation of the universe and the creation of man. It is *in the beginning,* during the historical week of creation, that God created Adam and Eve, that He instituted marriage, and that He put them in the wonderful garden. The words of

Jesus confirm the correctness of the literal interpretation, at least on the short duration of the whole creative work.

The source of our knowledge of God's way of creating

It is very perplexing to hear that the framework interpretation leaves to science the question of the length and sequence of the creative works of God. This raises the question of how we can know the way everything was created. By definition, science is the study of phenomena that we can observe, repeat, and subject to experiments in order to check the exactness of our hypothesis. The creative acts are past, finished, unique in history, impossible to repeat, and thus inaccessible to scientific experimentation. Moreover, these creative acts do not come from visible natural phenomena that the scientific investigation could grasp. They come from the invisible Word of God. Every true scientist, and especially every true Christian scientist, should remain very humble when he or she tries to contemplate the creation of the world. For science cannot say anything with certainty about origins.

Hebrews 11:3 says, "*By faith* we understand that the universe was created by the word of God, so that what is seen was not made out of things that are visible." It is by faith, and not by sight! If it is true for the fact of the creation itself, it is also true for the stages and the particular methods of the creative acts. Actually, the verb "to create" or "to form" (*katartizô*) in Hebrews 11:3 does not only teach us the fact that the world was created by God; it also informs us that He created in an orderly way. By faith, we understand that the universe was formed, put into order, and organized. It is not enough to believe that the world comes from God. We must believe the Word of God, which reveals to us the *architectural genius* by which God formed the world.

Since the Creator and Constructor of the world is the invisible Word of God, it is impossible for the human eye to have a scientific look at it and to carry out experiments on the sequence of the creative acts. No man has ever been an eyewitness of these past events. The only eyewitness is God Himself, which means that we depend entirely on His revealed Word. It is our only source of knowledge of these unique events in history. By faith we understand that "in six days the Lord made heaven and earth, the sea, and all that is in them" (Ex. 20:11).

Summing up this second part we conclude that the framework interpretation, including other similar figurative views, raises more problems than it solves. Its superficial literary analysis is not convincing. The dichotomies it establishes (between "refined style" and "literal meaning," between "thematic" and "strictly chronological," between "background" and "no chronological intent," between "meaning" and "facts," etc.) are artificial and do not faithfully give an account of the whole content of the biblical revelation. Its understanding of the seventh unending day is confusing and contradictory. It does not seriously take into account, and even contradicts, the rest of Scripture, especially the rest of Genesis as well as Exodus 20:8–11. Not only does the "traditional" literal interpretation have no need of being revised and changed, the new framework theory is constructed on weak and doubtful exegetical and theological bases. We concur with R. V. McCabe's conclusion:

> Therefore I conclude that the framework view poses more exegetical and theological difficulties than it solves and that the traditional, literal reading provides the most consistent interpretation of the exegetical details associated with the context of the early chapters of Genesis and the overall theological message of Scripture that has a bearing on Genesis 1–2.[198]

III

THE FRAMEWORK INTERPRETATION IS DANGEROUS

1

Doubts On What God Really Said

We must now take one more step in our analysis and try to discern the potential and real dangers of the framework interpretation and its other figurative variants. This is the objective of the third section.

The framework theory raises a serious question in our minds: Did God actually say, "Let there be light" (1:3), and did He also say, "Let there be lights in the expanse" (1:14)? If the first and fourth days are just two different ways of looking at the same creative act, if the fourth day is just a recapitulation of the first day, such a question is legitimate. Did God really speak *two* distinct creative words? Or did He speak only one word, which would be a kind of mixture of these two revealed words—one word whose real content is unknown? Or did He speak anything at all, and thus Genesis 1 would reveal to us just the *general idea* that God created everything?

Similar questions can be asked about the words that God spoke on the following days. Did God really say, "Let there be an expanse in the midst of the waters, and let it separate the waters from the waters" (1:6)? These questions are not clearly answered by the framework theory. This interpretation raises serious doubts in our minds on what God actually said during the creation week.

2

Rejection Of The Historicity Of Some Events[199]

Most of the framework proponents say they believe that God's creative acts revealed in Genesis are really historical. They vehemently protest against the suggestion that their theory attacks the historicity of these events. Here is one example among others:

> The Framework Interpretation affirms that God created all things from nothing and it affirms every aspect of the historical record in Genesis 1–11, against modern critical scholarship. Just because the days of creation may be arranged topically, rather than chronologically, does not in any sense mean that those things depicted as occurring on each day are not historical, even if Moses communicates this to us by analogy. No one who holds to the Framework Interpretation denies that by his word God created the heavens and the earth as well as all the creatures who fill them.[200]

In spite of those protests, serious doubts concerning the integrity of God's Word persist. It is one thing to *profess* the belief that the events "depicted as occurring on each day" are historical; it is another thing to really *maintain* this belief while still advocating the framework interpretation.

If the first and fourth days contain "a description of the *same event* from a different angle, with added information,"[201] then the following questions must be asked: Did the event described in Genesis 1:3–5, on the first day, really happen as an event? Did the other event described in Genesis 1:14–19, on the fourth day, really happen as an event? The answer of the framework position seems to be no. No, these *two* events did not happen *as events*. Genesis 1:3–5 and 1:14–19 do not narrate two distinct historical events, in spite of all the grammatical and semantic appearances. These texts would just reveal to us the *idea* that God created the light and the lights.

Besides, if the created realities, once supernaturally created, must be maintained only by "ordinary providential means," according to Kline's theory and others, this raises other similar questions. For example, did a *specific event* happen when God separated the waters under the earth from the waters above? We are constrained to say no. No, these waters, after they were created, needed only a normal providential act of cosmological process as observed today in order to be separated.

According to the clear teaching of the Bible, however, these waters were separated by a supernatural act never seen again today and produced by the authoritative Word of God alone who spoke these words once and for all. "And God said, 'Let there be an expanse in the midst of the waters, and let it separate the waters from the waters.' And God made the expanse and separated the waters that were under the expanse from the waters that were above the expanse. And it was so" (1:6–7). The separation of the waters into two parts was not a normal providential act of God after the waters were created but was the direct result of the supernatural creation of the expanse by God's powerful Word. This event *as event* is rejected by the framework interpretation, even though most of its proponents believe that "God created heavens and the earth as well as all the creatures that fill them," including the waters above and below.

Furthermore, according to Kline and others, the waters under the earth, once created and separated from the waters above, needed only the providential action of the sun as we know it today in order to slowly evaporate and to let the dry ground appear. But again, according to the clear teaching of the Bible, this created water was gathered by the Lord's authoritative Word alone in a supernatural act accomplished once and for all. "And God said, 'Let the waters under the heavens be gathered together into one place, and let the dry land appear.' And it was so" (1:9). The gathering of the waters under the heavens into one place was not a normal providential act of God after the waters were created and separated but was the direct result of God's supernatural formation of the dry land by the authoritative Word of God (see also Psalm 104:7–8). According to the framework interpretation, the events described on the second and third days did not really happen as *events*. We have in these verses only the revelation of the *idea* that God created the heavens, the seas, and the dry land.

Lastly, were the lights really created *in* the expanse? And was the expanse really created in order to *separate* the waters? In this case, it was necessary that the earth of verse 1 (mass of waters) be created first, then the expanse, then the lights; therefore the lights after the earth. This is contrary to Kline's framework theory, which says that the earth cannot have existed alone, by itself, "suspended in a spatial void," but once created, it would have needed to go through normal cosmological processes of formation of lights. This means that the events described on the first, second, third, and fourth days did not really happen as *events*. We have here only the *idea* that God created the earth, the expanse, the oceans, the dry land, and the stars.

J. B. Jordan actually affirms that the framework theory reduces the events of Genesis 1 to "ideas." He even discerns the pernicious influence of Gnosticism and of its tendency to reduce the historical events of Christianity to ideas.[202]

The framework interpretation must necessarily abandon as historical several events depicted as occurring on some days of the creation week. That is not to say that the framework interpretation denies that by His Word God created the heavens and the earth as well as all the creatures who fill them. But we must believe all that God said He did, not just the parts that we like, as is the case with the framework interpretation.

When the temporal points of reference are completely dissolved into the acid of this approach, which takes Genesis 1 figuratively, it is not surprising to see that the events recorded in these days are themselves eroded by this same acid. Even if one maintains the contrary is true, the framework theory does not only reject the historical reality of the days, it also rejects the historical reality of several events described on the first, second, third, and fourth days. The framework theory is subtle and insidious. The temporal frame is figurative, and the historical events recorded in this temporal frame seem to become more and more figurative, in spite of the vehement protests to the contrary. One wonders where this corrosive effect will stop.

3

More Corrosive Effects Of This Approach

We can see this deeper corrosive effect at work in Christopher R. Smith's book.[203] This other student and disciple of M. G. Kline uses the same framework approach as his professor but goes further. The same usual arguments in favour of the framework theory are promoted (the two-triad structure responding to two "deficiencies," the problem of the existence of light without the sun, the contradictions between Genesis 1 taken literally and Genesis 2, the poetic style of Genesis 1, Genesis 2:5 and the principle of ordinary providence, etc.). Smith adds nothing new in favour of the framework view. He does not interact with any of the many criticisms that were made during the past fifty years. He never quotes them or even alludes to them, as if nobody had ever put forward any critical examination of the theory. He simply stands in awe of the newly discovered comprehension revealed to him by the most insightful teaching of professor Kline. The difference in Smith's approach is that he builds on what his professor taught him, thus opening the door to all kinds of extremes. Speaking about the main way Kline influenced him, Smith says:

> His insightful reading of one text in particular, the account of the days of creation at the beginning of Genesis, changed forever the way I would understand that text, and the way I would henceforth read all others.[204]

For most of the main proponents of the framework view quoted so far, only the *length* and the *sequence* of the creation days are figurative. As for the *events* themselves reported on these days, they are, according to them, real historical creative events, even though we have demonstrated that such is not the case. We have seen that some of these events are, in fact, being seriously eroded and even rejected by this approach, which takes Genesis 1 figuratively, becoming just "ideas" rather than real events. At least most of the framework proponents want to maintain the historicity of God's creative acts reported in Genesis 1–2. That is not the result of their view, but that is at least their intent. With Smith, that is not the case anymore. Real time and real historical events disappear altogether. Time and historical events are so closely connected in God's plan for the world that it cannot be possible to remove one without sooner or later attacking the other. In Smith's book, we see how far the framework interpretation can lead, while being still strictly based on its classic teaching received from its main proponent in the twentieth century. Here are some of Smith's claims:

> Here was an amazing depth of meaning I had never appreciated before in the account of the days of creation. This passage was not so much a description of how we got here as an explanation of why we were here. It had a moral purpose, challenging humans to acknowledge God's supreme lordship, despite their pretensions to self-determination and self-sufficiency.[205]

> I had learned from Dr. Kline that the most important thing, whether we took the chapter literally or not, was to appreciate its moral message. We needed to witness and participate in the "Sabbath enthronement of God" as the

> culmination of creation. This account does not "cater to our curiosity" about origins, I insisted.[206]
>
> I entitled my course, "Genesis and the Human Condition," convinced by now that the purpose especially of these early chapters was to explain the brokenness of human existence as the cumulative result of alienation from God. My class, however, wanted to talk about "Genesis and Human Origins," since they were equally convinced that the purpose of the book was to tell us where we came from and how we got here.[207]
>
> But my main response was that if they really wanted to know why this account could not be understood as descriptive of actual events, even in a poetic way, they should return the next week.[208]
>
> The inescapable conclusion is that the early chapters of Genesis are not necessarily intended as "history," that is, they are not always attempting to portray, even in stylized form, actual events as they took place in the past. The point of these stories is primarily a moral one instead.[209]

Smith places before us a number of false dilemmas, similar to those posited by W. R. Godfrey. The first chapters of Genesis are not about the *how* but about the *why*. They are not about origins but about a moral message. They are not descriptive of actual past events but informative about the present human condition. This is what Smith learned from Kline. As Andrew Kulikovsky rightly says:

> Thus, God's actions in history are transformed into mere philosophical and theological motifs, and moral principles. This is exactly what the Framework Interpretation aims to do.[210]

Why can the Christian moral message not be based on historical facts and why can the Christian explanation of the present human condition not be based on precise past events that have really happened? These two things are closely connected in God's Word, but for our modern minds, illuminated by new exegetical tricks (or by modern secular scientific theories that make many Christians afraid to go against the current trends), they become "opposite" things impossible to reconcile.

Before Smith began his studies under Kline's guidance, he was an Evangelical Christian and a Young Earth creationist. His studies under Kline's tutelage have led him to a completely different understanding of Genesis. According to him, the days of creation are figurative, and the events reported in these days are no more real or historical than the days themselves. This is what he has learned from his seminary professor, he says, and there is no reason to doubt his word. Submitted to the care of Kline's teaching, Smith has discovered that the events of the creation week have disappeared altogether. Clearly the acid of this approach, which takes the days of creation figuratively, is destroying not only the time frame of the creation account but also the events themselves.

When ministers of the Word and theologians affirm that "No one who holds to the Framework Interpretation denies that by his word God created the heavens and the earth as well as all the creatures who fill them,"[211] this comment probably depicts correctly C. R. Smith's position. Although it is somewhat dubious that Smith really believes in a creation *ex nihilo*, it would be difficult to prove that he does not believe in some sense that God created the world and all that is in it. That does not mean that Smith's views are faithful to and respectful of God's Word. His views have been deeply influenced by modern liberal critical scholarship. One thing is certain: because Smith has "discovered" new insights from Kline's teaching, he now clearly rejects the fact that those things depicted as occurring on each day are historical. He holds these unbiblical views "just because" the days of creation are supposed to be arranged topically. He himself admits the close connection between his newly discovered framework view and his bold rejection of the historicity of many events of the creation account as revealed in Genesis 1. This rejection of the historical events is simply *the logical conclusion* of the several false dilemmas posited by the main framework and figurative proponents—false dilemmas identified and analyzed in a preceding chapter.

In short, when we read Genesis 1 and 2 through the lens of the framework view, the only food that is ultimately being left for us and for our faith is this: a moral message deprived of God's powerful and wonderful creative acts, a mere description of the present human condition—nothing more.

4

The Centrality Of The Present Reality

More must be said concerning the corrosive effect of the framework interpretation on this disciple of Kline. According to Smith, the Bible does not reveal to us how God created the universe. It simply tells us what pre-scientific men observed around them and what they (wrongly) thought about the origin of the world. Smith says that the Bible presents to us an "observational cosmology."[212] The "observer," the sacred writer of the book of Genesis, has not received a special revelation giving him information above or beyond the natural-scientific abilities of his own culture. Rather, he presents us with a phenomenological account, describing how things appeared to him and how they seemed to have been made.

> Could we not see Genesis 1 as a lyric meditation on the "finished product" of creation, a product that looked compellingly like "six days' work" to the observer? Three divisions: day and night, sky and sea, then the land. Three populations: of day and night, of sky and sea, then the land. And a seventh day of rest and worship, showing that this observer saw meaning and purpose in this ordered creation. Just like the descriptions throughout the Bible of a

> moving sun and a flat earth, this could have been intended literally by the original writer, and we could understand it as true from within an observational perspective: yes, this is how it looks as if all of this was put together.[213]

> We do not, therefore, need to believe that the biblical authors were given natural-scientific insights far beyond the capabilities of their cultures in order to maintain our faith in the Bible as the inspired word of God and our supreme authority in matters of doctrine and morals.[214]

> By now we should realize that Genesis, when understood as originally intended, does not present an objective scientific account of the origins of the universe. It rather presents a phenomenological account—that is, it describes how things appear and how they appear to have been made.[215]

The direction Smith is going helps us to see more clearly the path that his predecessors have taken before him, for they are basically on the same road. Smith is simply further along that road. They all try to understand the creation account of Genesis 1–2 *in light of the present reality*.

For N. H. Ridderbos, who popularized the framework view even before Kline published his first article on the subject, "the author expresses himself in terms derived from the world-picture of the ancient Orient, or to put it differently, in the terminology current in his day."[216] Ridderbos gives the example of the concept of a celestial arch, which separated the waters above, the heavenly ocean, from the waters beneath—a concept that Moses supposedly borrowed from ancient Orient mythology and incorporated into the creative account. Here we see again the influence of the critical way of thinking—as pointed out in a previous chapter—mingled with the framework view.

Then for Kline, the created realities, once created, are supposed to have been maintained only by normal providential means, as we see this providence at work today.

> The unargued presupposition of Genesis 2:5 is clearly that the divine providence was operating during the creation period through processes which any reader would recognize as normal in the natural world of his day.[217]

Thus, Kline does not clearly distinguish God's creative acts during the days of creation and God's providential acts once His creative activities were finished. Besides, the fourth day is seen as a recapitulation of the first day because the existence of the light without the sun is contrary to our present experience. According to Futato, our knowledge of the real world signals an overlay of day one and day four. He asserts that there must be such an overlay, since "light without luminaries is not part of the real world in which the original audience lived."[218] Similarly, the alternation of day and night during the first three days is said to be impossible without the sun and the moon because those days and nights must be understood in light of our normal days and nights today. The whole week of the creation account is consequently taken figuratively.

A further consequence is that God did not create the world in six days, nor has He given us a model to follow during the rest of history. Instead, He is supposed to have used the present reality of our six days of work and one day of rest as model for His "picture frame classification" of creative events. As Blocher says, "the human writer used a stereotype from his cultural milieu in presenting the creation in the form of the week."[219] Noel Weeks strongly criticizes this idea according to which the present reality governs the way God has revealed His works of creation. He considers this issue no less than a matter of true or false religion.

> It is often said that the creation is described in seven days because this is the pattern of labour to which the Hebrews were accustomed. The text however says the very reverse. The Hebrews are to become accustomed to a seven-day week because that is the pattern that has been set by God. Rather than God being made to conform to an already

> established human pattern, man must conform to the pattern that has been set by God. The point is an important one as it is crucial to the distinction between true and false religion. The oft-repeated claim that human thought and custom has created the categories through which, of necessity, all God's activity must be viewed is a denial of the spirit of biblical religion. It gives to man the priority which rightly belongs to God.[220]

Then, for Futato, the reality of the pagan idolatry that reigned in Canaan during the time of Moses and Israel is supposed to have determined and limited the purpose of God's creative account. He does not see God's redemptive purpose in the life of Israel in light of God's initial creative plan. Rather, he sees God's creative acts in light of God's redemptive work in the context of the worship of Baal in Canaan.[221]

W. R. Godfrey falls into the same trap when he says this about the second day and about Genesis 1 in general:

> Here we see Moses giving a description of God's creative act from the perspective of what the common man sees and experiences in this world. Genesis 1:6–8 is not a detailed scientific description of reality but a presentation of what we see. We see that there are lower waters on the earth and upper waters that produce rain. We also see that between those waters is a space that Moses called the firmament or expanse that we would call the sky. That separation of waters and that expanse is what God brought into being on the second day. . . By describing the creation on day two in terms of human perspective, God reminds us again that Genesis 1 is for us. The character of the revelation is not to tell us about creation in the abstract but about the appearance and meaning of creation for God's image bearer.[222]

What Godfrey says about the second day is simply impossible. Godfrey himself tells us on the next page that

"God does not declare his acts on the second day as good" because "God had not completed his work on the waters. . . The work on the waters is not completed until the third day." Waters covering the whole world before there is any dry land is not what the common man sees and experiences in this world today. God's creative activities on the second day are not a description of our present reality but a description of what God really did on that day, and what He did was not yet completed. It was completed only when "the earth was formed out of water and through water by the word of God" (2 Peter 3:5). In this passage, the apostle Peter does not interpret the creation account as a presentation of what we see but as an explanation of what God really did.

Similarly, for Smith, "Genesis 1 is a lyric meditation on the 'finished product of creation.'" It is "true from an observational perspective," and "it describes how things appear and how they appear to have been made." According to Smith, these "insights" come directly from Kline's teaching. His former professor led him on the "right" path. Ultimately, all these proponents of the framework and figurative views walk on the same road. In short, for them, *the present reality* is the key to our understanding of the creation account.

Does the Bible really present an "observational cosmology"? Of course, the original creative acts of God have produced works that can still be observed today or that have a deep effect on us today. We see birds flying, fish swimming, and animals walking because on the fifth and sixth days God created the birds, the sea animals, and the land animals, which have multiplied in abundance since that time. We see trees and plants around us because on the third day God created the vegetation, which has been very fruitful since that day. But it is something very different to say that Genesis 1 is simply a reflection of the world that Moses observed around him (with all the scientific limitations of his culture).

For example, to which present reality do the deep water and the Spirit hovering over the deep correspond? What did Moses see in nature around him that was similar to that deep water and to that hovering Spirit? Did he see something similar to the separation of the waters or to the formation of the continents? And what about the perfect holiness of Adam and Eve? What about the wonderful garden of Eden and the perfect harmony between God and His creatures, and between husband and wife? What about the vegetarian diet prescribed to both animals and man? Moses certainly did not see any of these realities around him in Egypt, or in the desert amidst a rebellious people, not even in the promised land of Canaan, where God revealed Himself as the Lord of rain, vegetation, and life. It is interesting to see that Jesus, who read and explained the Genesis account, could say to those who wanted to divorce: "But from the beginning it was not so" (Matt. 19:8). Christ took Genesis 1–2 as a simple description of the conditions that were in the beginning and that are no more. Certainly, according to our Lord and Saviour, Moses received a special revelation fundamentally different from the natural-scientific knowledge of his time and culture.

When we read the book of Exodus, and especially the events that happened at Mount Sinai, we see that Moses had at his disposal much more than the cosmological concepts of his culture. God revealed Himself to Moses face to face on the mountain. God even directly wrote the Ten Commandments on stone with His own finger (Ex. 31:18; Deut. 9:10). Among these Ten Commandments that He gave, the fourth commandment says, "For in six days the Lord made heaven and earth, the sea, and all that is in them, and rested on the seventh day. . ." (Ex. 20:11).

In this case, we may confidently say that we actually have here an "observational cosmogony" rather than an "observational cosmology." We have a factual record of the origin of the universe, true to what the divine author observed when He progressively accomplished His own works of creation, rather than a description of the present characteristics of the universe the way the human author may have observed them. The Almighty God who wrote the text of the fourth commandment Himself certainly wrote from the point of view of an observer—the Observer being the Lord Himself. After all, He is the Creator of the universe. He was there in the beginning. He saw exactly everything He made and how He made it. His scientific knowledge of the origin of the world is absolutely perfect and totally exhaustive. He was able to say to His servant Moses many more things than what He wrote on the rock and many more things than the cultural environment of Moses could know at that time as well—things that Moses wrote in the first chapters of the book of Genesis, for instance.

Thus it is of great importance whether we are affirming that God was made to conform to an already established human pattern or that man was obligated to conform to the pattern that has been set by God. Noel Weeks is certainly right when he says, "The point is an important one as it is crucial to the distinction between true and false religion."

5

The Deceptiveness Of The Word Of God

It is true that the Bible does not always speak in a "scientific" way, and we should be thankful that this is so. For example, the Bible does not say that the earth rotates on its axis and travels around the sun at such and such a distance or speed. Rather, it says that "the sun rises, and the sun goes down" (Eccl. 1:5). When the Bible speaks that way, however, it does not deceive anybody. When we still speak in that manner today, we do not deceive anybody either. Even the great modern scientists and meteorologists of our time say that the sun rises, moves in the sky and goes down, and everybody understands them perfectly. Their information is exact, precise, and easy to understand – much more than their incredibly complex hypothetical modern cosmologies.

When I say to my wife that I am going to take a walk after the sun sets, I do not deceive her in any way by saying that. She does not need any mathematical formula or explanations of the movements of the planets, stars, and galaxies for that purpose – neither the ones elaborated by Copernicus, Galileo, or Kepler, nor those imagined by more modern big bang cosmologists. It would be extremely difficult and risky to use those highly sophisticated and hypothetical explanations to inform your wife or your neighbour about the time of the day you do an activity or about your location on the earth.

Truth according to the Bible is highly relational and interpersonal. The ninth commandment does not require us to avoid uttering any word that is not "objectively scientific." That would simply be impossible to do. The ninth commandment requires that we do not bear false witness against our neighbour (Ex. 20:16).

When we read the creation account in Genesis 1, the text itself claims to present to us the original creative acts of God. The author of Genesis does not say, "Here is my own description of how things appear to be or seem to have been created, from my limited point of view." He says, "In the beginning, God created the heavens and the earth. The earth was without form and void, and darkness was over the face of the deep. And the Spirit of God was hovering over the face of the waters. And God said, 'Let there be light,' and there was light. . ." (1:1–3). The whole first chapter of Genesis exclusively says what God said, what He separated, what He made, what He named, and what He deemed good. The human author was perfectly aware of the fact that man was not there when the Spirit of God was hovering over the face of the deep, or when God created the light, or during any of the works made on the first five and a half days, when the earth was not yet ready to receive its human inhabitants.

C. R. Smith admits that the author is convinced that he is describing actual facts, yet, at the same time, Smith believes that the author is erring.

> Unlike Paul, the Genesis author does not seem to be aware of the limitations of his own knowledge. In other words, not only does he not know; he does not know that he does not know. While his description of creation and cosmology is phenomenological, he believes it to be objectively accurate. Moreover, his readers would have understood it as such, and his fellow biblical authors certainly did: as we have seen, the rest of the Bible follows

> this same observational cosmology. Nowhere in the Bible is it "corrected."[223]

It is very clear that, according to Smith, the biblical text, from cover to cover, deceives us and deceives all its readers about its description of God's creative works and its cosmology. In other words, he claims that the Bible is not true in all that it says. For example, Moses, guided by the Holy Spirit, would have deceived us (unintentionally) when he said that God created an expanse to separate the waters above from the waters under the expanse:

> Which cosmology would you prefer to use as a springboard for your quest to understand the origin and nature of the universe and the origin and diversity of life on this planet? The naïve observational cosmology of Genesis, with its solid sky, "waters above," pushed-back seas and light without the sun? The geocentric Aristotelian cosmology? That of Copernicus, with its perfectly circular planetary orbits? Some other cosmology? Or our present understanding of the nature and structure of the universe, which, while admittedly still subject to refinement, nevertheless incorporates all of the objective observations and measurements made over the centuries into a reasonable working model?[224]

Faced with such intellectual intimidation, the reader is not left with much choice. Yet nothing less than the witness of Moses about God is called into question. Did Moses truly witness in favour of God, or did he bear false witness against God? Did God really say? Did God really make? Did God really separate? Did God really see what Moses says He saw? In such a critical perspective, the answer is obviously no, of course not! At least, this is what the idol of secular science tells us. Unintentionally, Moses deceives us, claim its proponents. And what about God Himself? Does He deceive us too? Yes, indeed! He did so when He wrote the Ten Commandments on a stone with His own finger, when He said that He created the world in six days and rested on the seventh day. Can you imagine?

This means that the Lord would have borne false witness against Himself, that He would have sinned against His own ninth commandment, that the prophets and the apostles would have continued on the same path, and that Christ Himself would have borne false witness against His Father. "The rest of the Bible follows this same observational cosmology. Nowhere in the Bible is it 'corrected,'" says Smith. Jesus would have then misled and deceived His people when He said that "from the beginning of creation, God made them male and female" (Mark 10:6). The Word of God would have been deceiving the Church for about twenty centuries, until man incorporated "all of the objective observations and measurements made over the centuries into a reasonable working model." According to this approach, one would have to conclude that what the Bible says about God's creative acts is nothing but a false witness against God Himself.

Moreover, in such a view, the third commandment is also transgressed: "You shall not take the name of the Lord your God in vain, for the Lord will not hold him guiltless who takes his name in vain" (Ex. 20:7). If Smith is right, then the prophet Moses, Christ, and the apostles would have borne false witness against God and taken the name of the Lord our God in vain, grieving the Holy Spirit, who inspired Moses and all the biblical writers. This means that, on Mount Sinai, God Himself would have borne false witness against Himself, that what He wrote on hard stone was actually a lie. This is inconceivable. "God never lies" (Titus 1:2). "God is not man, that he should lie" (Num. 23:19). "It is impossible for God to lie" (Heb. 6:18). "The testimony of the Lord is sure, making wise the simple" (Ps. 19:7). Smith attacks the infallibility of the Word of God and tarnishes the glory of God and of His Son Jesus Christ. Moreover, if Christ had sinned against any of the Ten Commandments, even only once, our eternal salvation would be lost forever. With respect to the creation account, this means that we must accept this account as true and factual because God has told us so in His Word. As Christ acknowledged to the Father: "Your word is truth" (John 17:17).

6

A "Pre-Scientific" Solid Heavenly Dome

Smith gives some examples of what he calls "observational cosmology." The idea of a solid sky has already been mentioned. This example illustrates very well the hermeneutical tendency that is being propagated nowadays, especially about the creation account of Genesis. Here are other things that Smith says about that presumed dome:

> The "heavens" or "sky" is a dome stretched out like a canopy to keep out the "waters above" and create a habitable space beneath: "God made the dome and named it 'sky'" (Gen. 1:7–8).[225]

> When we take these statements literally—as it has often proven difficult for literally-minded interpreters to do—they have profound cosmological implications. According to the Genesis account, God's creative activity on the second day consisted of inserting a hollow but solid dome-shaped object in the midst of the waters, with the result that some of the waters were then "below" this dome while the rest were "above" it. The Hebrew word for this object is *raqiya*, derived from a verb meaning "to spread out" or "to beat metal thin." The King James Ver-

> sion renders this word as "firmament," and the NIV as "expanse," but a solid object is definitely in view. The picture is of a tent being stretched out on poles, or of metal being poured or pounded into the shape of a dome. This was the Hebrew understanding of how God had made the sky.[226]

According to Smith and many others, if we accept literally this old Hebrew understanding of how God made the sky, we would evidently be totally mistaken. Today we *know* from science that the sky is not a solid dome, and that the Bible and its pre-scientific cosmology are then plainly wrong. What should we think about this biblical *raqiya* (or *raqia*)? Danny Faulkner wrote a book on cosmology and creation in which he addresses this matter. His analysis is much more cautious and respectful of God's Word. Considering the fact that several commentators seem confused or skeptical about the true historical and cosmological reality of the expanse of Genesis 1, it is worth quoting at length here the very informative notes made by Faulkner about this famous expanse.

> Therefore those who accept the big bang and make it part of their Christian apologetics are guilty of interpreting the Bible in terms of current science. This is a very dangerous precedent. However this sort of attitude is not new. For instance, the translators of the Greek Septuagint (LXX) rendered the Hebrew word *raqia* as *stereoma*, which Jerome followed as *firmamentum* in the Latin Vulgate, which in the AV (authorized, or King James Version) was transliterated as *firmament*. This is a terrible translation, and many modern translations break from this to render *raqia* as expanse. The word *stereoma* conveys the meaning of something hard, such as the crystalline spheres of ancient Greek cosmology upon which the stars were implanted. Thus, the translators of the LXX incorporated the current cosmology of their day into their translation. This is very

similar to those who wed the big bang to the Genesis creation account today.[227]

In the Bible (Genesis chapter 1) the Hebrew word that is usually translated 'heaven' is *shemayim* [sic]. A related word is the Hebrew word *raqia*, which was discussed in an earlier chapter. There it was pointed out that this was badly translated as 'firmament' in the AV. Firmament gives the meaning of being hard, and was actually introduced in the LXX as an accommodation of ancient Greek cosmology. The word *raqia* is a noun that comes from a verb meaning 'to beat out' as one might do to a metal. Gold is so malleable that gold working is a good example of this process. Hammers or rollers may be used to pound gold into a thin leaf that is only a few atoms thick. Gold leaf can be applied as a coating to surfaces in a process called gilding. Therefore, the *raqia* is something that is beaten out.

Obviously, the *raqia* must have some property of something that has been beaten out, but just what is that property? Some people who support the rendering 'firmament' argue that the thing being beaten out is usually a metal, and since hardness is a common metallic property, the *raqia* must be something hard. However, there are other metallic properties, such as luster and electrical and thermal conductivity. Why should we restrict the meaning to hardness? Furthermore, gold is one of the best examples of a metal that is beaten out, but gold is not known for hardness. Perhaps the important property is not anything inherent in the thing beaten out but rather is a result of the process itself. When something is beaten out, it is stretched, so the *raqia* could be something that is stretched. This is especially interesting in that the Old Testament has numerous statements of the heavens being stretched out, as in Psalm 104:2. In fact, just these passages provided some inspiration to Russ Humphreys for his model. If we understand the stretching of the heavens to mean the expansion of the universe, either past or present, then the Christian should welcome redshifts, not oppose them.

Many modern translations of the Bible follow this lead in rendering *raqia* as 'expanse.' In Genesis 1:14 the stars are said to be in the *raqia* of the *shamayim*, and in Genesis 1:20 birds are described as flying in the *raqia* of the *shamayim*. Thus a good alternate meaning may be the sky. In English we say that both birds and stars are in the sky. In other passages the heavens (*shamayim*) and the expanse (*raqia*) are equated. For instance, Genesis 1:8 explicitly states that God called the '*raqia*' *shamayim*. Therefore, the *shamayim* and the *raqia* may be used interchangeably. If this is correct, then there may be no basis for always making a distinction between the two – the two may be used as variety to mean the same thing or may refer to different aspects of the same thing. In any case, it is very clear that the *raqia* is not something hard.

Some people think that the creation of the *raqia* refers to the creation of space itself. If this is true, then what are we to make of the statement in Genesis 1:1 that says that God created the heavens (*shamayim*) at the very beginning? Others think that the creation of the *raqia* on the fourth day [Faulkner surely means 'on the second day' – P. B.] refers to the creation of the earth's atmosphere. If this is true, then what are the waters above the *raqia*? Proponents of the canopy theory (that there was a large volume of water above the earth's atmosphere before the Flood) think that the *raqia* is the earth's atmosphere and that the water above was the canopy that was collapsed at the time of the Flood. Others think that this water refers to atmospheric water in the form of vapor and clouds. Still others think that there is a large amount of water beyond the space that we see in the universe. At least a few creationists think that the *raqia* is the creation of the crust of the earth or the earth's surface. This interpretation is dif-

> ficult to square with some of the other considerations just discussed. We have no definitive answers on just what is meant by these passages, and so some latitude in speculation on this is allowed. However, the best interpretation is that space itself was created in the first verse with the creation of the heavens.[228]

Thus, there is no need to see this *raqiya* as a solid dome, and consequently as being part of an old incorrect pre-scientific view of the cosmos. We may not always understand all the details presented in the biblical account of creation. God's works are profound and mysterious. We cannot claim to fully or exhaustively comprehend God's work of calling creation into existence. This does not mean that this revealed account is false or deceiving. On the contrary, if they walk humbly before the Lord and take His Word seriously, the Christian scientists will find new insights for their research and may even make interesting contributions to their own scientific field. If God says that He made an expanse, who are we to say that this act of creation as described in His Word is not true? After all, the Bible is the authoritative and infallible Word of God and is entirely true and trustworthy in all that it says.

7

A False View Of God's Accommodation

Considerable time has been spent analysing some aspects of the teachings of one of Kline's disciples. Since C. R. Smith's position is not shared by all the framework proponents, it is time to come back to the main proponents of the framework and figurative views and to raise some more concerns that apply to the framework interpretation in general. In any case, Smith's views demonstrate that beginning with the framework hypothesis can indeed start one onto a slippery slope of various heretical ideas.

It is often argued by people who adopt the framework and the figurative interpretations that their approach to Scripture is similar to that of John Calvin. They speak about Calvin's principle of God's accommodation to our human understanding so that what the Bible says can be clearly understood throughout all time by all people. To justify their own view and to attempt to make it look like a solid Reformed position, they say that Calvin's scriptural view on creation was that it has been written in the language and culture of the Near East at the time of writing. J. A. Pipa summarizes it well:

> This "framework hypothesis" views the days of creation as God's gracious accommodation to the limitations of human knowledge—an expression of the infinite Creator's work in terms understandable to finite and frail human beings.[229]

First, God always accommodates Himself to our limited human capacity whenever He reveals Himself. This is true of all of Scripture and takes nothing away from the reality of what is recorded. God never makes untrue statements and never deceives us even as He accommodates Himself to our limited human understanding. Second, is the description aforementioned really reflects how Calvin depicted God's accommodation to us? Would God limit His accommodation to the text and language of Scripture? If so, it would mean that what God says in Scripture is not necessarily true and reliable but simply understandable by ancient Near Eastern people or by us. Any reader of Calvin's commentary on Genesis will soon discover that this is not what Calvin meant by his "principle of accommodation." According to Calvin, God did not simply accommodate His *Word* to past or present culture; He also accommodated His *works* to us. In his commentary on Genesis 1:5, Calvin wrote:

> Here the error of those is manifestly refuted, who maintain that the world was made in a moment. For it is too violent a cavil to contend that Moses distributes the work which God perfected at once into six days, for the mere purpose of conveying instruction. Let us rather conclude that God himself *took the space of six days, for the purpose of accommodating his works* to the capacity of men.[230]

This concept is clear and simple. According to Calvin (against Augustine), God really created the world in the space of six days so that we may grasp, contemplate, and imitate His creative works. Therefore, what God says in Genesis 1 is not only understandable to anybody, it is also true for all times and cultures. What He says corresponds accurately to what He really did in the beginning, and what He did was made in a way that is accommodated to our capacity. He did not speak only in order to be understood (and later on to be corrected by men). He spoke in order to be understood *and believed*. Calvin's insights are certainly worthwhile, but one must be careful not to misrepresent his view. Yes, indeed, when God created the world, He "took the space of six days, for the purpose of accommodating his *works* to the capacity of men." This is a rich and profound affirmation.

W. R. Godfrey quotes this preceding sentence from Calvin's commentary on Genesis, yet wrongly concludes that "the result of our limited capacity is that God must accommodate *himself* to us when he *reveals himself*."[231] Concerning Calvin's commentary on Genesis 1:31 (God taking pleasure in His creation after His creative work is completed), again Godfrey says that "the meaning of the text is clear, but *the words* of the revelation are accommodated to our capacity."[232] He has a similar comment on God's rest. "He does not need to rest, but we do. He is accommodating *his revelation* of his creating work to us and our needs."[233] In his summary of Calvin's principles of interpretation, Godfrey concludes that Calvin's second principle is: "Recognize that in the text God is accommodating *himself* to our capacity."[234]

Godfrey fails to recognize that, according to Calvin, God is accommodating both His Word *and His works* to our capacity. Godfrey admits that "the interpretation of Genesis 1 presented in our study does not reach the same conclusion as Calvin on the days of creation,"[235] but he does not seem to see that he reaches a different conclusion precisely because he does not fully apply Calvin's principle of accommodation. Godfrey applies this principle to God Himself and to His words but not to God's *real works* of creation and to God's *real activities* at the end of the week of creation.

> There is a vital difference between Calvin's principles as actually worked out by Calvin himself, and Calvin's principles as interpreted by Godfrey. It is not *in the text* that

> God is accommodating Himself, according to Calvin; it is in His very *work*. There is no distinction made by Calvin between God's actual work and the recording of that work in Scripture.[236]

The proponents of the figurative interpretation precisely lack Calvin's wisdom and simplicity in the way they understand God's accommodation to us. If God's creative acts are spread over billions of years, it is very difficult to see that it is an accommodation of His works to the capacity of men. How many people can grasp, contemplate, and imitate God's creative works if these works have been made in such an incredibly long period of time? The number of zeros after the first digits becomes meaningless to our finite and frail minds. If God really worked that way, how can His creative works be understood throughout all time by all people? One may discern another kind of accommodation here. It is the danger of accommodating God's Word to the claims of secular science and to a modern atheistic view of the origins of the world.

8

God's Inability To Communicate Accurately

When the Bible uses figurative language, it usually does so with an express purpose, so that we might understand its meaning. For example, we think of the prophetic gestures in the Old Testament, the parables in the Gospels, or the stars, the lampstands, the trumpets, and the seals in the book of Revelation. The text itself shows us that they are figures. These figures have a precise meaning. They are used with the purpose of revealing a truth that is useful for us. A yoke is a picture of the bondage under the oppression of neighbouring nations. A boiling pot announces the impending judgment of God. "The kingdom of God is *like* a seed," "the seven stars *are* the angels of the seven churches, and the seven lampstands *are* the seven churches," etc. There is a *correspondence* between the image and the reality, and our intelligence enlightened by the Holy Spirit may know and grasp the meaning of this correspondence.

What about the figurative interpretation of Genesis 1? To which meaning or reality do the days refer? If the week of creation is a figure, what does it represent? The answer that we hear from the framework proponents is rather hopeless. In fact, we simply do not know its meaning. These days are "divine days."[237] They represent the "heavenly time" in which God reigns and acts, but this heavenly time has no sequential or chronological connection whatsoever with "earthly time."[238] Ultimately, we cannot know anything about it.

In other words, the days of creation may represent anything *except* six literal, sequential, earthly days. We do not know what they represent, but we know for sure that they do not represent an earthly temporal week! Frankly, what good does it do to us that God revealed His creative work by a figure that in the end does not mean anything for ordinary Christians? "In the Bible analogical and metaphorical explanations to God have to communicate a clear revelation of God or they are useless."[239]

It has been noticed several times by critics of the framework interpretation that this approach empties the word "day" of any meaning. God seems unable to communicate accurately what He wants to tell us. Trying to interpret Genesis 1 becomes a hopeless enterprise. The truth revealed by God becomes impossible to grasp. One may still say that God reveals the truth to us, but the interpreter can never be reasonably sure that he understands what the author meant.

9

"Heavenly Time" And Complete Skepticism[240]

Irons and Kline are sensitive to the critique raised in the preceding paragraphs and reply that the days refer to an objective reality. Kline developed the complex theory of a "two-register cosmology," apparently with this concern in mind. According to this view, the language of the lower register (days, evenings, and mornings) is used metaphorically to point to realities pertaining to the upper register. In response to E. J. Young's criticism of A. Noordtzij and N. H. Ridderbos (who say the figure of the days does not correspond to any reality), Irons and Kline say that the days are as real as the "upper register" to which they pertain. But what does that solve? There is no proof that the heavenly days have a rhythm that moves at a different speed than the earthly days, or that they are ordered according to a different sequence than the earthly days.

When the glorious cloud of the Lord came to fill the tabernacle (Ex. 40) and to dwell with Israel, we see a precise *temporal synchronism* between heaven and earth. The same is true when this glory left the temple to go to Babylon with the exiled (Ezekiel). When God and Satan talked about Job, and when the angels visited the earth to execute God's will and to meet with His earthly servants (Abraham, Daniel and his friends, the shepherds of Bethlehem, the women at the grave, etc.), we find the same temporal synchronism between heaven and earth.

When Christ ascended into heaven and sat at the right hand of the Father, when He stood up to receive His servant Stephen into His glory, when He acts powerfully from heaven in favour of His Church on earth, when He sends judgments on earth (according to the book of Revelation), and when He will come back from heaven in all His glory, the events happening in heaven and on earth are again temporally synchronized.

God is not bound by time. He created time and uses it for His purpose but is Himself eternal. Being eternally the same, He is also the God of the covenant. According to this covenant, He comes and walks in *earthly time* with His people. When God confirmed His covenant with Abraham in Genesis 15, He used very specific language regarding time. Abraham's offspring would be afflicted in a land not their own for 400 years. Such a covenant, with its promises and threats, would mean nothing if heavenly time in which the Lord reigns had no correspondence with earthly time. Christ's departure from the earth, His ascension into heaven, and His session at the right hand of the Father on His throne of glory would have no significance for our salvation, for the gathering work of the Church, and for the destiny of the world.

Such an idea of "heavenly time" disconnected from earthly time cannot but lead the Church of the Lord on the road to skepticism. We cannot know with certainty anymore whether the work God does from His heavenly throne has any significance for us today.

> Speaking more broadly, one wonders how far Kline will take his two-register cosmogony. Ultimately, if carried to its logical conclusion, it leads inevitably to total skepticism because all that can be known about God occurs within the upper register.[241]

Besides, how can we know which elements of Genesis 1 pertain to the upper or to the lower "register"? In the beginning, God indeed created what we may call a cosmological duality, heaven and earth (1:1). After that, it is specifically the *earth* that is lit, formed, and filled. Godfrey makes this correct observation:

> While the "two-register cosmology" is present in Scripture, it is not clear that it is a helpful key with reference to the days of Genesis 1. Genesis 1:2 focuses our attention on the earth, not on the heavenly realm. From that focus follow the days of Genesis 1, which are all about the creation of the visible world, including the creation of day itself.[242]

On the first day, God entered into the earthly creation and worked in the earthly creation by His Spirit hovering over the face of the waters. On the first day, the light was created. It was separated from the darkness, exactly as on the second day the waters were separated into two parts, and exactly as on the fourth day the day and the night were again separated by the visible lights. On the first day, the light and the darkness received names ("day" and "night"), just as on the second day the expanse received a name ("heaven"), and just as on the third day the dry land and the waters received names ("earth" and "seas"). The waters, the earth, and the seas are earthly realities and are not presented as metaphors of heavenly realities any more than the light, the darkness, the day, and the night, which are described the same way as *earthly realities*. The evenings and the mornings are measured by the light, then by the lights inside the earthly visible realm. The evenings and the mornings are as much part of the earthly realm as the trees, the fish, and the humans.

> If the framework argument about the two-register time is so clearly intended by the Holy Spirit, why is it that

> the literal words 'day,' 'evening' and 'morning' are never used this way anywhere else in Scripture?[243]

Moreover, how could the evening, the night, and the darkness serve as metaphors for "heavenly time"? The Bible does not say that there are nights and darkness in heaven. It never mentions that there is an alternation of evenings and mornings in heaven. Right from the beginning, heaven was completely formed and filled with perpetual light, whereas God acted toward the earth in six days in order to light, form, and fill the earth, and to give the earth a rhythm of days, nights, and weeks peculiar to the earthly realm.

> Kline rightly argues that when God's Glory Cloud appears, it is the heavenly realm inserting into the earthly. But this means that God marches in earthly time along with his people. . . Thus, even if there were two kinds of time, God chooses to come into earthly time and move with it. And since Genesis 1 has to do with the lightening, forming, and filling of the *earth,* it has to do with *earthly* time.[244]

Consequently, it is invalid to assume that a two-register spatial view of cosmology implies that time also has a two-fold scheme. J. B. Jordan has shown that the framework theory mixes up the characteristics of time and of space. We can appreciate the soundness of his analysis:

> Kline assumes that the bipolarity of space—heaven above and earth below—implies a bipolarity of time and days—heavenly days and earthly days. But this is to misunderstand completely the difference between time and space. Heaven is the spatial model for the earth, and it is spatially "above," or apart from, the earth. The first week is the temporal model for all weeks to come, but it is not "above" these other weeks; rather it is *before* all later weeks. The contrast is not between heavenly days and earthly days, but between the first days and later

days, the first week and later weeks. Heaven relates to earth as archetype; the first week relates to later weeks as prototype. The first week took the same length of time in both the heavenly and earthly realms, and given how it is described in Genesis 1 (a sequence of normal days with evenings and morning [sic]), it took the same span of time as all later weeks. Heaven is a real place, and so is the earth. The first week was a real week, and so are all later weeks.[245]

10

The Lack Of Clarity Of Scripture

Quite often the framework proponents reply to those who criticize their position: "You have not understood correctly," "You do not accurately present our position," "Your criticism does not respond to the point that we make."[246] This may be true in some cases[247] (although many critics are to the point), and if so, we have to humbly correct what we have said in error, acquire a better understanding of their view, and try to appreciate or criticize more accurately if needed. Yet one of the problems with the framework view is precisely that a clear and simple passage of Scripture is reinterpreted in such a complex manner that only those with intellectually superior minds can, apparently, understand it. "Its sophistication makes it difficult to understand and, consequently, difficult to refute."[248]

An ecclesiastical committee, which had the task of studying the different interpretations given to the days of creation (and who was open to these different interpretations), has come to this conclusion about the framework interpretation:

> The Framework view is the most easily misunderstood of the options. Proponents should recognize that it is com-

> plex, it has sometimes been poorly expressed, and it does not answer every exegetical question.[249]

Well trained and knowledgeable ministers of the Word of God humbly admit this concerning Kline's writings:

> The second aspect of his theory is called two-register cosmogony. Now I have to admit that I read this material a number of times, but was unable to figure out exactly what is meant. It is very complicated. It is very abstract. It is very far removed from the simple statements of Genesis 1. That in itself ought to send up warning signals to anyone who loves God's Word.[250]

> I sincerely wonder whether many of the adherents of Kline's position have been so in awe of his scholarship, incredible knowledge of Hebrew, and overall devotion to the Scriptures that they have accepted his position without being fully being able to comprehend, let alone to answer, the overwhelming and bafflingly complicated intricacies of his language and argumentation. I certainly cannot. Many times I did not know "whether I was coming or going."[251]

The Reformers of the Church have firmly believed and proclaimed *the perspicuity* of the Word of God. Believers who read the Bible do not depend on specialists in science or theology for the understanding of the main message of the Bible. This does not mean that there are no difficult passages to interpret or that the Church does not need the help of theologians or specialists. But when the believers read and study the Bible, humbly submit to the Word, and ask for the guidance of the Holy Spirit, the Word of God is then a lamp to their feet and a light to their path (Ps. 119:105). "The Word is very near you. It is in your mouth and in your heart..." (Deut. 30:14; Rom. 10:8). Believers are able to judge, and they are called to judge every doubtful interpretation of Scripture (1 Cor. 2:15; 1 John 2:20). "On the contrary, the

Framework, with all of its sophisticated argumentation, relegates understanding of the opening chapter of the Bible to the intellectual elite."[252]

Godfrey is right when he says that "the authority of the Bible is at stake when some interpreters suggest that Genesis 1 is not true or reliable or clear in its meaning."[253] However, his own figurative view of the days (actual for us, figurative for God, not a timetable of God's actions but a model timetable for us to follow) is not much clearer than the classic framework view.

The framework theory definitely confuses the meaning of Scripture, puts a veil on its clarity, and takes it away from our mouths and our hearts.[254] And yet, it is difficult to imagine a use of language in Genesis 1 that could more clearly communicate that the universe was made in the space of six days.[255] "Just suppose that God really did mean to communicate creation in six ordinary days, how could He have done so more clearly?"[256]

If God has not really created the world in six consecutive days, we should then accuse God of having deceived His people for thousands of years. The framework interpretation does not just try to offer a "better" understanding of the days of creation. It is a view diametrically opposite to the way the Church has almost universally understood Genesis until the time when attempts were made to harmonize the Bible with the theory of long geological periods and the theory of evolution.[257] Apparently, humble servants of God and the little ones in the Church cannot understand by themselves anymore the meaning of the Word of God. They should definitely close the Holy Book and leave it up to the specialists.[258]

11

A Source Of Division In The Church

The Bible has been written both for the simple and for the learned in the Church. The Word of God is both *clear* and *profound*. Its style communicates a message to us that is within every believer's reach; at the same time, its literary refinement gives the opportunity for the scholarly to study for hundreds of (literal) days, months, and years, never exhausting all of its richness. There is something in it for everybody, for the little ones and for the erudite, but normally, the two should come to the same conclusion. Fundamentally, the text has the *same meaning* for the simple and for the learned.

It is obvious that the framework theory is a source of division. On one side are the simple, who have not understood the deep, hidden meaning of the first chapters of Genesis, but are condemned to remain at the simple straightforward meaning of the text; on the other side are the learned, who have been enlightened. It seems that the framework theory has the tendency to develop a "two-register church" (to adapt M. G. Kline's "two-register cosmology"). How is it possible that a small minority of theologians and ministers understand the deeper meaning of Genesis 1, but the vast majority of other believers never perceived it for two thousand years of church history? It is very sad to see this division in the Church.

12

The Pervasive Influence Of Modern Secular Science

The framework proponents want to assure us that their interpretation is based strictly on exegetical considerations, but to no avail; in several specific cases we discern the *pervasive influence* of modern naturalistic scientific theories.[259] They say they have the desire to be based only on Scripture, and we do not doubt their sincere desire to be faithful to the Word of God. But the phenomenon before us is somewhat similar to a compass that still has the characteristics of a compass but is disturbed when approaching a perturbing magnetic field. For example, H. Blocher says this:

> The rejection of all the theories accepted by the scientists requires considerable bravado. It may be said that the work of many neo-catastrophist writers [i.e. those who believe in a global Flood and a young earth – P. B.] shows courage, not ignorance. Nevertheless, current opinions, built on the studies of thousands of research scientists who keep a very close eye on one another, continue to look very probable. Anyone rejecting them is taking an immense step. One must be absolutely sure of one's ground, especially since the neo-catastrophic hypothesis

> raises formidable objections. One must be sure that the text *demands* the literal interpretation.[260]

Then he says, "This hypothesis [the framework theory] overcomes a number of problems that plagued the commentators," and one of these painful problems, according to him, is "the confrontation with the scientific vision of the most distant past." He adds:

> So great is the advantage, and for some the relief, that it could constitute a temptation. We must not espouse the theory on the grounds of its convenience but only if the text leads us in that direction.[261]

This sentence is so true, but in front of the painful problem of "the confrontation with the scientific vision" and of allegedly "all the theories accepted by the scientists," the temptation remains great. Kline is even more affirmative:

> But if the exegete did not have the light of Gen. 2:5, he would certainly be justified in turning to natural revelation for possible illumination of the question left open by special revelation. And surely natural revelation concerning the sequence of developments in the universe as a whole and the sequence of the appearance of the various orders of life on our planet (unless that revelation has been completely misinterpreted) would require the exegete to incline to a not exclusively chronological interpretation of the creation week.[262]

Thus, for Kline, the Bible does not reveal anything about the stages of creation. "Natural revelation" (meaning, for him, the way modern secular scientists understand nature) would *require* the exegete to listen to another source of authority. In short, this approach gives an undue esteem to modern scientific theories. Kline says:

> The conclusion is that as far as the time frame is concerned, with respect to both the duration and sequence of events, the scientist is left free of biblical constraints in hypothesizing about cosmic origins.[263]

According to this view, the Bible allows complete scientific freedom on two points: the duration and the sequence of the events of creation. On the contrary, we should all submit to the lordship of God concerning these two points that are clearly revealed in Genesis, no matter how much self-renunciation it costs. "The Framework Hypothesis is an ingenious attempt to allow the Genesis text to fit the opinions of modern secular science."[264]

It is sad to see Kline's negative attitude towards his brothers and sisters who hold to a young earth, while he candidly admits that his own interpretation does not contradict the theory of evolution:

> In this article I have advocated an interpretation of biblical cosmogony according to which Scripture is open to the current scientific view of a very old universe and, in that respect, does not discountenance the theory of the evolutionary origin of man. But while I regard the widespread insistence on a young earth to be a deplorable disservice to the cause of biblical truth, I at the same time deem commitment to the authority of scriptural teaching to involve the acceptance of Adam as an historical individual, the covenantal head and ancestral fount of the rest of mankind, and the recognition that it was the one and same divine act that constituted him the first man, Adam the son of God (Luke 3:38), that also imparted to him life (Gen. 2:7).[265]

Hearing these surprising assertions, some have asked legitimate questions to Kline:

> Which side are you on, anyway?. . . Where has this man been? Has he been all by himself, tied to his ivory tower

> of theological speculation? Does he not know the terrible toll that evolutionism and its various forms of accommodation have taken?[266]

As observed by John Byl, Godfrey has a negative attitude similar to Kline's toward the literal interpretation, which is apparent in his defence of the figurative view.

> Why is Dr. Godfrey so insistent, regarding science, that "all truth is God's truth" and that "ultimately a true reading of the Bible and genuine conclusions of science will be compatible"? And why does he associate the defense of literal creation days with "a retreat into anti-intellectualism"? Such statements indicate that his reading of Genesis 1 is not isolated from "scientific" and "intellectual" concerns.[267]

Godfrey further says that "many Christians have sought ways to isolate themselves from the evil and degeneration they sense around themselves," and "have sought to create a subculture of their own." In this context, he describes the creation science movement as "a manifestation of withdrawal," "an anxious response that is a form of circling of wagons tightly for protection and preservation," an "anti-intellectualism and inappropriate rejection of science." "When it is taken too far, it is dangerous and unbiblical," he says.[268]

This harsh general judgment is a very unfortunate and unfair judgment that is not documented and not based on any specific case evaluation. One wonders which "anti-intellectual" creation science brothers he has read, and in which way their position is dangerous and unbiblical. It would certainly be dishonest to apply such a judgment of "anti-intellectualism" to at least the eight Christian scientists holding the literal interpretation cited in this study.[269]

Actually, many mainstream secular scientific organizations and magazines consider creationists such heretics, outcasts, and untouchables that they totally refuse to hire them or publish their works, or even quote them and enter into debate with them. Discrimination against those who question evolution is systematic and comprehensive. Persecutions of competent scientific "Darwin Doubters" by the modern academic Inquisition is well known and documented.[270]

How can one dare to say that creation scientists withdraw, isolate themselves, protect themselves, and reject science? The reality, in this context of discrimination, is that they conduct researches in a wide variety of scientific fields, most of the time with no government funding. They review and comment on the most recent works from secular scientists. They make their thoughts and the results of their own research known through all kinds of books, magazines, videos, movies, conferences, museums, and web sites, both for learned people as well as for the general public and families.[271] Theologians and pastors – who generally do not have much scientific training themselves – should think twice before they despise these brothers who often sacrifice a brilliant scientific career for the cause of the truth of Genesis 1.

T. S. Beall suggests that there are two primary reasons why so many evangelicals have abandoned the literal day view or become agnostic on the whole matter. Neither of these reasons has anything to do with the exegesis of Genesis 1.

> The first reason is that many evangelicals are convinced of either evolutionary theory or (at the least) the geological evidence for the age of the earth. . . The second reason is that they are somewhat embarrassed by [the six 24-hour day view]. They, too, want to be known as reputable scholars, not simply knee-jerk fundamentalists. And what could be more "fundamentalist" than insisting on a literal six 24-hour day creation for Gen 1? Such an opinion is regarded as anti-intellectual and anachronistic: in the words of Richard Dawkins, those who hold such a view are simply dismissed as "clowns"![272]

In spite of the vehement protests of many of those who promote this position, the framework theory represents a dangerous concession to modern anti-Christian scientific theories. John MacArthur observes:

> The framework hypothesis is the direct result of making modern scientific theory a hermeneutical guideline by which to interpret Scripture. The basic presupposition behind the framework hypothesis is the notion that science speaks with more authority about origins and the age of the earth than Scripture does. Those who embrace such a view have in effect made science an authority *over* Scripture. They are permitting scientific hypotheses—mere human opinions that have no divine authority whatsoever—to be the hermeneutical rule by which Scripture is interpreted.[273]

These words are not exaggerated. Framework adherents usually claim that their goal is simply to provide the best exegesis of the Genesis text in light of the findings of modern scientific research. Still, Tremper Longman III, another promoter of the framework view, wrote:

> Scientific research concluded that the world is old, the process that brought the cosmos into being took huge amounts of time, and that human beings are relative latecomers to the process and are themselves the product of a long evolution. It seemed that scientific models of creation clashed with the biblical description. But did they really? Some theologians immediately adopted an apologetic stance and tried to sow doubt concerning the validity of the scientific model. However, cooler heads raised the question of the interpretation of Genesis 1–2. They used the new discoveries as an occasion not to review the truth of the Genesis account but to review whether the traditional interpretation was correct.[274]

Longman comes close to inadvertently admitting that the harmonistic views are a result of trying to marry the text with science. Instead, he claims that the developments in science caused interpreters to rethink Genesis 1. As a result, the "cooler heads" developed what he believes is the proper view. He went on to add:

> It appears that Genesis itself is not interested in giving us a clear and unambiguous understanding of the nature of the creation days. This ambiguity fits in with the overall impression we get of the passage, that it is not concerned to tell us the process of creation. Rather it is intent on simply celebrating and asserting the fact that God is Creator.[275]

The same false dilemma than the ones heard earlier is again being used to reject the veracity of the historical process of creation clearly revealed in Genesis 1. Why all these theologians uncritically repeat in unison the same false arguments aimed at rejecting the plain, straightforward meaning of the holy Word of God?

Clearly, the framework interpretation leads to all kinds of unbiblical compromises, including theistic evolution and progressive creation. C. R. Smith is a good example. Bruce Waltke—who adheres to both theistic evolution and the framework interpretation—candidly admits that the framework theory is a theory "promoted to reconcile the Genesis account of creation with evolution."[276] The case of Howard Van Till is another well known illustration of this fact. During the 1980s, Van Till, now emeritus professor of physics and astronomy at Calvin College in Michigan, introduced the Christian Reformed Church (CRC) to the possibility that evolution was the process God used to create the heavens and the earth. His views expressed in his book *The Fourth Day* have caused quite a stir in the CRC. The first five chapters of his book presenting "The Biblical View" draw heavily on the works of N. H. Ridderbos and

Meredith Kline for his literary framework hypothesis. This leads him to say:

> The seven-day chronology that we find in Genesis 1 has no connection with the actual chronology of the Creator's continuous dynamic action in the cosmos. The creation-week motif is a literary device, a framework in which a number of very important messages are held. The chronology of the narrative is not the chronology of creation but rather the packaging in which the message is wrapped. The particular acts depicted in the Story of the Creator are not the events of creative action reported with photographic realism but rather imaginative illustration of the way in which God and the Creation are related.[277]

There is nothing new under the sun! The same line of reasoning is repeated again and again, with familiar key words like "no chronology," "literary device," "messages," and the now famous "not. . . but. . ." What is very telling is that Van Till seeks to interpret the creation account with this hypothesis, combined with a view of science biased toward an evolutionary model of origins. Even though Van Till does not like the term "theistic evolution," he holds to a form of theistic evolution, which he calls "creationomic perspective." He believes that God created everything with built-in capabilities to adapt and evolve into whatever is required by the situation.[278] Clearly, the framework theory has given him the opportunity to reconcile the Genesis account of creation with evolution. More recently, Van Till's belief in evolution has led him to reject the Reformed faith and supernaturalism altogether and to adopt pantheistic beliefs and process theology.[279] The fact that Van Till has now rejected any faith in a personal God casts a particularly unfavourable light on his former position.

Today, Calvin College has fully embraced evolution and the CRC has opened the door for the full-scale promotion of evolution and its far reaching theological implications. This requires major revision of key doctrines, including the infallibility of the Bible, the historicity of Adam and Eve, original sin, Christ's atonement, election and eternal punishment.[280] Once the teaching of the framework interpretation has pierced the dam, the high pressure of conformity with evolution immediately rushes into the hole and rapidly produces its destructive effects.

Another framework proponent, J. A. Thompson, declared:

> But the method by which God achieved all this is not given. Was it by the separate instantaneous creation of each and every creature? Or was it by some process which, in the case of living things, began with some simple organism and arrived finally under the hand of God at the completed product, that is by some evolutionary process? In my view, the narrative in Genesis 1 yields no information about the divine method, only that, whatever the method, it was divine, so that any concept of purely naturalistic evolution without God is ruled out. But there are alternatives to the two extreme positions of fiat creationism and naturalistic evolution, and men of deep Christian conviction can be found who hold such intermediate positions as theistic evolution or progressive creationism.[281]

The depth of people's Christian conviction is not the issue here. Christian commitment is not the standard for truth; God's Word is. Sadly, it seems that Thompson considers the traditional interpretation of Genesis 1 as being "extreme." Also, Thompson is plainly wrong when he says that Genesis 1 "yields no information about the divine method" of creation other than that God was responsible for it. Longman is wrong too when he says that Genesis 1 "is intent on simply celebrating and asserting the fact that God is Creator." Our study has shown that Genesis 1 reveals much more—a magnificent historical process of creation that is evident at first glance even for a child. God spoke several things into existence in a precise order and majestic progression in the space of six days. Moreover, plants and animals would only bring forth "after their kind" (Gen. 1:11, 12, 21, 24, 25). This common phrase completely eliminates the possibility of any evolution from one "kind" of creature into another.

Timothy Keller is another example of a Christian leader who has accepted the framework theory and uses it for promoting the synthesis between Genesis 1 and the theory of evolution, which he falsely describes as "science." Keller is the influential pastor of Redeemer Presbyterian Church (PCA) in New York City. He believes human life was formed through evolutionary biological processes and promotes this idea for apologetic purposes, in order to reach out the skeptics and atheists more easily. In his paper presented at the first BioLogos workshop held in November 10–12, 2009, in New York City, he concludes:

> Even though in this paper I argue for the importance of belief in a literal Adam and Eve, I have shown here that there are several ways to hold that and still believe in God using evolutionary biological processes. [282]

Keller partly justifies his position on the claim that "the author of Genesis 1 did *not* want to be taken literally." "Perhaps the strongest argument for this view," he says, "is a comparison of the order of creative acts in Genesis 1 and Genesis 2." The way he expresses this comparison is typical of the framework proponents' arguments (the supposedly poetic nature of Genesis 1, the relation between day one and day four, their interpretation of Genesis 2:5, their belief that no vegetation on earth could have been created before there was rain).[283] According to *The BioLogos Forum* website, this first BioLogos workshop:

> . . .was co-sponsored by the Rev. Tim Keller, pastor of Redeemer Church in New York's leading evangelical fellowship. This meeting sought to build bridges and enable comfortable communication channels between respected

> evangelical scientists working on origins and key religious leaders in the evangelical Christian church.[284]

Darrel Falk, president of BioLogos, adds that:

> The scientists [at the workshop] likely all held the position that God has created life in a manner that is consistent with the findings of mainstream science. . . We talked about how evangelicalism's approach to the science/faith issue has sometimes served as an artificial barrier that blocks some from entering the realm of faith.[285]

BioLogos is an organization that promotes the idea "that evolution, properly understood, best describes God's work of creation." Most of their contributors have rejected biblical inerrancy and the historicity of Adam and Eve. Timothy Keller is associated with them and has given them an exegetical and a theological justification of their evolutionary views.

In France and French-speaking Europe, there is a similar connection between theologians accepting the framework view and Christian scientists promoting theistic evolution. Lydia Jaeger, professor at the Evangelical Seminary in Vaux-sur-Seine, near Paris, and director of studies at the Bible Institute in Nogent-sur-Marne, also near Paris, has fully embraced the framework theory taught by her former professor Henri Blocher. Jaeger simply repeats Blocher's arguments in favour of the literary (framework) interpretation. She says that Blocher's book *In the Beginning* is *the* "reference book on the subject,"[286] without mentioning any of the several theologians who have criticized the framework view during the past fifty years. Jaeger has founded an association of Evangelical scientists called *Réseau des scientifiques évangéliques* (RSE), and is a member of the board of directors of this association, which aggressively promotes theistic evolution.[287]

Like Keller and BioLogos, Jaeger and the RSE adopt theistic evolution for apologetic purposes. They believe that this synthesis between the Bible and the secular theory of evolution will help render the Christian faith more acceptable in the opinion of unbelievers, disregarding how unbiblical such a synthesis is[288] and how damaging it has been in mainline churches during the past hundred and fifty years or so.

Thus, more and more, we see the generation of pastors and theologians who have been taught or influenced by professor Meredith Kline take an open unbiblical theistic evolutionary stance and use the framework theory as an exegetical justification, which opens the door to any secular theory on the origins of the universe and life. As Blocher has pointed out, when Christians are plagued by the painful problem of the confrontation with the atheistic scientific vision of the most distant past, it is obviously tempting to espouse the framework theory on the grounds of its convenience. In doing so, the Church is accommodating to the world spirit of the age. For that reason, Noel Weeks suspects that the real debate surrounding the interpretation of the first chapters of Genesis is not hermeneutical at all.

> The real problem is that we as Christians have in a double sense lost our historical perspective. We have forgotten that the church has always been under pressure to allegorize Genesis so that it may conform with Plotinus or Aristotle or some other human philosophy. We have treated the problem as though it were a modern one, as though we alone have had to face the onerous task of holding to a view of cosmic and human origins which is out of sympathy with the philosophical premises of our culture. The second sense in which we have lost our historical perspective is that we have forgotten that until our Lord returns we face strife and conflict in this world. We have sought to avoid that conflict in the intellectual realms. We have accepted the claim of humanistic thought that its scholarship is religiously neutral when the Bible teaches us that no man is religiously neutral. Man either seeks to suppress the truth in unrighteousness or to live all his life

> to the glory of God. In that total warfare scholarship is no mutually declared truce.[289]

Another sad consequence is a "Genesis apathy" in the Church.

> One of the most frustrating effects that the Framework Hypothesis has had on the Church is that many Christians have been led to believe that Genesis 1 is unimportant. Ever since the early 1800s the Genesis accounts of the Creation and the Flood have been under constant attack. Sadly, many Christians are apathetic because they have been led to believe that it is nothing more than a side issue. Yet this is one of the most important battles the Church can be fighting at this time since this is where the secular society has been attacking. The Framework Hypothesis bears some of the responsibility for this since it actually attempts to downplay the biblical text.[290]

13

The Origin Of Our Seven-Day Week

Finally, the framework theory raises a very simple but persistent question: Where does our present seven-day week come from? What is its origin? Many framework proponents try to explain the origin of the creation account in the form of a week by suggesting that it is a stereotype borrowed from the human writer's cultural milieu, as we have seen. The seven-day week existed as fact in the Middle East during Old Testament times, and the biblical writer used it to present the creation in the form of a week.

The man-centred logic of this approach is obvious. Again, the present reality of the biblical writer is used as an explanation for the way God revealed His creative acts. But what explanation is given about the origin of our seven-day week? Apparently, we do not know who imposed this weekly rhythm on Moses' cultural milieu and how it was imposed on them. But what does the Bible say?

As opposed to this man-centred religion, Scripture says, "Six days you shall labor, and do all your work, but the seventh day is a Sabbath to the Lord your God. On it you shall not do any work. . . For in six days the Lord made heaven and earth, the sea, and all that is in them, and rested the seventh day. Therefore the Lord blessed the Sabbath day and made it holy" (Ex. 20:9–11).

The Bible presents a God-centred approach easy to understand. The way God created heaven and earth and all that is in them is the explanation for the fact that our life is governed by the rhythm of a seven-day week. God's creative acts in six days followed by a day of rest is the origin of our six days of work and one day of rest. Apart from this divine explanation, there is no way we can know the origin of our seven-day week. If God did not really create in six days, followed by a seventh day of rest, which He blessed and sanctified, how could man copy his Creator and follow His model?

CONCLUSION

We have studied in detail the arguments propounded by the advocates of the framework interpretation and other figurative views; we also have taken into consideration the responses given by their opponents. We conclude that the framework interpretation and other similar figurative theories are not faithful to Scripture and thus must be rejected.

In the *first* part, we have seen that the objections raised against the literal interpretation do not stand in light of a serious study of the text. Literary refinements such as the cardinal number of day one, the definite article of day six and day seven, and the absence of evening and morning on day seven are in complete harmony with the literal interpretation. Besides, day four is not a recapitulation of day one but reveals both a historical continuity and a clear progression from the creation of the light to the creation of the sun, the moon, and the stars. This strongly supports the literal interpretation. The different use of the word "day" in Genesis 2:4, meaning "when," does not change the clear meaning of the days in Genesis 1.

Moreover, the "evidence" from Genesis 2:5–6 to which the framework interpretation appeals is totally baseless. This text does not contradict a literal reading of Genesis 1, neither does it teach that God used only ordinary providential means to sustain His creation during the creation week. Maintaining such a line of reasoning inevitably leads to the rejection of several creative acts revealed as real historical events in Genesis 1. Thus, Genesis 2:5–6, as well as Genesis 2:19, are in full harmony with the literal interpretation.

In the *second* part, we have observed that the framework and figurative interpretations are problematic in several ways. The so-called structure in two triads as well as the literary structure based on the "problems" mentioned in Genesis 1:2 are not textually based but have been superimposed on the text. These alleged literary forms of Genesis cannot be a solid basis for questioning or denying the true literal and historical reality of the days of creation. In order to do so, the proponents of the framework and figurative interpretations have introduced a potentially disastrous dichotomy between literary form and chronological data, as well as a very dangerous dichotomy between meaning and history. When we get rid of such false dilemmas, we can only conclude that Genesis 1 does not present sequentially disconnected topics, nor a pattern for work meant to teach us lessons disconnected from a true and accurate account of actual chronological events. On the contrary, it reveals a magnificent and masterly historical progression of God's creative acts to the glory of God alone. At the end of this magnificent work, the Lord has blessed and hallowed the seventh day—not an unending day that contradicts other assertions of the framework proponents, but a day of normal length set aside as a day of rest for man.

Besides, it cannot be proven that the background of Genesis 1 is the entrance into Canaan, and that the author of Genesis had no intent to reveal a chronological and sequential order of the days of creation. To the contrary, Exodus 20:8–11 tells us clearly that the people of Israel were commanded to give rhythm to their weekly activities in their new life in Canaan, according to the pattern that God had given them when He created the world in six days and rested on the seventh day. Sound exegesis requires that the word "day," in the two parts of the commandment, be taken in the same sense in both instances. According to the analogy of faith, the rest of Scripture also contradicts the framework interpretation. The whole book of Genesis, including its genre, outline, and content, fully supports a literal interpretation. In the whole Pentateuch, the word "day," when associated with consecutive ordinal numbers, always has a literal sequential meaning. Similarly, the language of "evening and morning" clearly points to nothing else than literal days.

Christians must not be ashamed to confront secular scientific theories with what God has clearly revealed in Genesis 1 about the length and sequence of His creative acts. After all, God was the only eyewitness of these unique and majestic events. The revelation of these events as reported in the Bible is our only source of information on His creative activities.

In the *third* part, we have noticed several dangers related to the framework interpretation. It persistently casts serious doubts on what God really said in the beginning. It attacks in an insidious manner what God has clearly revealed about the creation of the world, specifically about the length and the sequence of the days of creation. In spite of vehement protests to the contrary from framework proponents, their views necessarily reject the historicity of several events that happened during the week of creation, especially during the first four days.

The disastrous and far reaching corrosive effects of this approach are sadly seen in C. R. Smith's book (Smith is one of M. G. Kline's disciples). When such extreme theologians maintain that we must reject the cosmogony of Scripture on the basis of modern scientific insights, they boldly and unashamedly assert that the Word of God deceives us. Even though the "fathers" of the theory do not seem to go that far, ultimately, all the framework proponents walk on the same road. For them, the present reality is the key to our understanding of the creation account. The logical conclusion down this road is the rejection of the historical events of the creation account. Taking the present reality as our starting point clearly contradicts the Scriptures, which tell us that the biblical authors have received a special revelation fundamentally different from the natural-scientific knowledge of their time and culture.

For this reason, some framework proponents claim that the Bible errs and deceives us when it speaks of cosmological realities, thus directly attacking the infallibility of the Word of God. For example, they say that Genesis 1:6–8 speaks of a "pre-scientific" solid heavenly dome. When we analyze the word *raqiya,* however, there is no need to see it as a solid dome. This word may correctly be translated by "expanse."

John Calvin's view of God's accommodation is sometimes quoted in support of the theory, but Calvin simply confirms the validity of the literal interpretation by asserting that "God himself took the space of six days, for the purpose of accommodating his works to the capacity of men."

The framework and figurative views make it impossible to really grasp the true meaning of the days of creation and thus seriously undermine God's ability to communicate accurately. More particularly, Kline's two-register cosmology, with its "heavenly time" disconnected from "earthly time," leads inevitably to complete skepticism because all that can be known about God occurs within the upper register. The framework theory reinterprets a clear and simple passage of Scripture in a very complex and abstract manner, thus relegating our understanding of the Bible to the intellectual elite. The Scriptures become hopelessly unclear and obscure for the ordinary reader. This irremediably leads to a division in the Church between the "simple" and the "learned" people.

Even though the framework and figurative proponents usually claim that their views are strictly based on exegetical grounds, it is obvious from their own words that many of them have been subjected to the pervasive influence of modern secular science. Several of these proponents use the framework theory to promote a false synthesis between the atheistic theory of evolution and the biblical doctrine of creation. Even the origin of our seven-day week becomes obscure, because it cannot be explained from the clear and simple biblical perspective anymore. It is of great importance whether we are affirming that God was made to conform to an already established human pattern or that man was obligated to conform to the pattern that has been set by God. The point is an important one as it is crucial to the distinction between a man-centred religion and a God-centred religion.

In conclusion, I encourage pastors, elders, theologians, educators, Christian scientists, and churches to exercise cautious and courageous discernment and to reject this false interpretation, even though it may mean for them the loss of their "academic credentials" or "respectability" before the secular world. The framework interpretation and its derivatives may seem attractive to some intellectual and academic people afraid of being labelled as "anti-intellectualists." This approach may also seem neutral or inoffensive to some ecclesiastical bodies, which have already been deeply contaminated by the teaching of its proponents. On the contrary, not only are these views useless for the edification of the Church, they also lead to all kinds of unbiblical compromises, including theistic evolution and progressive creation. Moreover, they are pernicious in the long term, for our faith and for our Christian witness to the world. May the Lord give us wisdom and insight, and may He, by His grace, keep us faithful to His Word.

ENDNOTES

1. Paulin Bédard, "Critique de l'interprétation 'cadre' ou 'littéraire' de Genèse 1," *La Revue Réformée* 252 (November 2009/5) 21–84, also available at http://larevuereformee.net/articlerr/n252.

2. The main authors in favour of the framework interpretation who have been considered in this study are N. H. Ridderbos, B. Waltke, M. Kline, L. Irons, H. Van Till, H. Blocher, M. Ross, M. D. Futato, R. S. Ward, W. R. Godfrey, and C. R. Smith (see the bibliography). Blocher also quotes M. J. Lagrange, B. Ramm, D. F. Payne, and J. A. Thompson in favour of this theory. R. V. McCabe adds M. Throntveit. He also mentions V. P. Hamilton, R. K. Hughes, C. J. Fredricks, G. J. Wenham, and R. F. Youngblood, who provide support for this interpretation while not attempting to provide a full defence of the framework view.

3. For example, I think of G. C. Aalders, E. J. Young, J. A. Pipa, D. F. Kelly, J. B. Jordan, G. F. Hasel, D. W. Hall, N. Weeks, A. S. Kulikovsky, F. Walker, K. L. Gentry, M. Zylstra, J. C. VanDyken, J. Sarfati, R. V. McCabe, M. J. Kruger, and others, who, for that matter, have been very useful for the preparation of this study (see the bibliography). J. C. VanDyken is surprised that Dr. Kline, the main advocate of the framework theory in North

America, has always refused to answer the criticisms of professor E. J. Young in 1962, convinced that his position was biblical and that it did not have to be defended anymore; see J. C. VanDyken, "The Framework Hypothesis," *The Trumpet* 12:4 (April 2000) 8.

4. The framework interpretation of the creation account of Genesis 1 has produced many reactions and commotions in Reformed and Presbyterian churches in North America during the past two decades and will likely continue to be a cause of great concern in the future. In 1985, the Reformed Churches in the United States (RCUS) took a strong stand against the framework interpretation and other non-literal views, confirmed at their Synod in 1999. The Synod of the Orthodox Christian Reformed Churches (OCRC) did the same in 1999. In 2000, the General Assembly of the Presbyterian Church in America (PCA) adopted a report allowing several views of the creation account, including the framework view. The General Assembly of the Orthodox Presbyterian Church (OPC) did the same in 2004. In 2001, the Synod of the United Reformed Churches (URCNA) affirmed that the Scriptures teach that God created all things good in six days defined as evenings and mornings, but failed to speak clearly and to address specifically the framework hypothesis. Since these different decisions have been made, ongoing debates on this issue continue to trouble the PCA, the OPC, and the URCNA. More recently, the Canadian Reformed Churches (CanRC) have requested the URCNA to clarify their stand on the framework interpretation. There are also ongoing debates on the web and in the magazines of these different federations. In Europe, the framework interpretation has become widespread in many Evangelical and Reformed churches.

5. It is the judgment of the report of the committee of the RCUS, *The Days of Creation*, section "Framework

Theory" that says that this theory is the most insidious, available at http://www.rcus.org.

6. In his introduction to his analysis of the framework theory, J. C. VanDyken sounds this warning by giving some examples of churches in Europe and in North America that rushed into unbelief after having succumbed to the influence of the Darwinian theory of evolution, "The Framework Hypothesis," *The Trumpet* 12:1 (January 2000) 7–9.

7. Lee Irons & Meredith G. Kline, "The Framework View," *The Genesis Debate: Three Views on the Days of Creation* (Mission Viejo, CA: Crux Press, 2001), 225.

8. Marc Kay, "On literary theorists' approach to Genesis 1: Part 1," *Journal of Creation* 21:2 (2007) 73, also available at http://creation.com/images/pdfs/tj/j21_2/j21_2_71-76.pdf.

9. H. Blocher, *In the Beginning: The Opening Chapters of Genesis,* trans. David G. Preston (Downers Grove, IL: Inter-Varsity Press, 1984), 51.

10. Meredith G. Kline, "Because It Had Not Rained," *Westminster Theological Journal* 20:2 (May 1958) 146–157, also available at http://www.asa3.org/ASA/resources/WTJ/WTJ58Kline.html.

11. M. G. Kline, "Space and Time in the Genesis Cosmogony," *Perspectives on Science and Christian Faith* 48:1 (March 1996) 2–15, also available at http://www.asa3.org/ASA/PSCF/1996/PSCF3-96Kline.html.

12. Irons & Kline, "The Framework View," 219. For a good summary of M. Kline's position, see J. C. VanDyken, "The Framework Hypothesis," *The Trumpet* 12:3 (March 2000) 4–9, and 12:4 (April 2000) 5–8.

13. L. Irons & M. Kline, "The Framework Response" [to the 24-Hour View], *The Genesis Debate: Three Views on the Days of Creation* (Mission Viejo, CA: Crux Press, 2001), 85.

14. W. Robert Godfrey, *God's Pattern for Creation* (Phillipsburg, NJ: Presbyterian & Reformed, 2003), 51–53, 81, 93. These five "problems" will also be discussed in this study.

15. Since the argument of the "two-register cosmology" is too broad to be analyzed in this paper and would need a more extensive study of the rest of Scripture, I will limit my comments on this view to some concerns in the last part of this study.

16. Quoted by Tas Walker, *Famous Evangelical Apologist Changes His Mind,* available at http://www.creation.com.

17. R. S. Ward, *Length of Days in Genesis,* section 2.3, available at http://www.spindleworks.com/library/ward/framework.htm.

18. These three Bible quotations are my translation.

19. J. A. Pipa, "From Chaos to Cosmos: A Critique of the Non-Literal Interpretations of Genesis 1:1–2:3," in *Did God Create in Six Days?*, ed. Joseph A. Pipa & David W. Hall (Greenville, SC: Southern Presbyterian Press, 1999), 183.

20. According to R. V. McCabe, "A Critique of the Framework Interpretation of the Creation Account (Part 1 of 2)," *Detroit Baptist Seminary Journal* 10 (2005) 53–54. Many very serious studies on the use and the significance of the word "day" in the Bible and in Genesis in particular have been presented. For example, one

may consult: J. Stambaugh, "The Days of Creation: A Semantic Approach," *CEN Technical Journal* 5:1 (1991) 70–78; G. F. Hasel, "The 'Days' of Creation in Genesis 1: Literal 'Days' or Figurative 'Periods/Epochs' of Time?," *Origins* 21:1 (1994) 5–37; J. Sarfati, *Refuting Compromise: A Biblical and Scientific Refutation of "Progressive Creationism" (Billions of Years), As Popularized by Astronomer Hugh Ross* (Green Forest, AR: Master Books, 2004), 67–105; R. V. McCabe, "A Defense of Literal Days in the Creation Week," *Detroit Baptist Seminary Journal* 5 (Fall 2000) 97–123. All these studies conclude that the days and the week of creation of Genesis 1 must be understood literally and not figuratively.

21. Ward, *Length of Days in Genesis*, section 2.3.

22. Godfrey, *God's Pattern for Creation*, 70.

23. J. Sarfati, "The Numbering Pattern of Genesis: Does It Mean the Days are Non-Literal?" *Journal of Creation* 17:2 (August 2003) 60–61. Sarfati quotes A. Steinmann, "*'ehad* as an ordinal number and the meaning of Genesis 1:5," *Journal of the Evangelical Theological Society* 45:4 (2002) 583–584.

24. For a more detailed argumentation in favour of the seventh day as a normal day, even if it does not end with the expression "evening and morning," see Pipa, "From Chaos to Cosmos: A Critique of the Non-Literal Interpretations of Genesis 1:1–2:3," 167–169; J. A. Pipa, *From Chaos to Cosmos: A Critique of the Framework Hypothesis*, available at http://www.westminsterreformedchurch.org/ScienceMTS/Science.Pipa.Framework.Critique.htm; Sarfati, *Refuting Compromise*, 82–84; B. Shaw, "The Literal Day Interpretation," in *Did God Create in Six Days?*, ed. Joseph A. Pipa & David W. Hall (Greenville, SC: Southern Presbyterian Press, 1999), 217; A. S. Kulikovsky, *A Critique of the Literary Framework View of*

the Days of Creation, available at http://hermeneutics.kulikovskyonline.net/hermeneutics/Framework.pdf, 11–13; M. Zylstra, *Revisiting the days of creation. . . again!*, section "Do these problems really exist?," available at http://spindleworks.com/library/zylstra/framework.htm; R. V. McCabe, "A Critique of the Framework Interpretation of the Creation Account (Part 2 of 2)," *Detroit Baptist Seminary Journal* 11 (2006) 108–117; see also Godfrey, *God's Pattern for Creation*, 60.

25. *The Report of the OPC Committee to Study the Framework Hypothesis*, presented to the Presbytery of Southern California (OPC) at its meeting on October 15–16, 1999, section II, C, available at http://www.asa3.org/gray/framework/frameworkOPC-SC.html; M. Ross, "The Framework Hypothesis: An Interpretation of Genesis 1:1–2:3," in *Did God Create in Six Days?*, ed. Joseph A. Pipa & David W. Hall, (Greenville, SC: Southern Presbyterian Press, 1999), 121–122, 128; H. Blocher, *Révélation des origines* (Lausanne: Presses Bibliques Universitaires, 1979), 48.

26. Lee Irons, "The Framework Interpretation: An Exegetical Summary," *Ordained Servant* 9:1 (January 2000) 9.

27. McCabe, "A Critique of the Framework Interpretation of the Creation Account (Part 2 of 2)," 109–110. McCabe also refers to K. L. Gentry, Jr., and M. Butler, *Yea, Hath God Said? The Framework Hypothesis/SixDay Creation Debate* (Eugene, OR: Wipf & Stock, 2002), 62.

28. *Ibid.*, 114.

29. K. L. Gentry, Jr., "Genesis Creation: Literal or Literary?" *Chalcedon Report* 452 (May 2003), also available at http://www.banneroftruth.org/pages/articles/article_detail.php?473.

30. Some arguments presented here have been developed by: E. J. Young, "The Days of Genesis" (second article), *Westminster Theological Journal* 25:2 (1963) 159–162; Pipa, "From Chaos to Cosmos: A Critique of the Non-Literal Interpretations of Genesis 1:1–2:3," 174–179; Pipa, *From Chaos to Cosmos: A Critique of the Framework Hypothesis;* J. B. Jordan, *Creation in Six Days: A Defense of the Traditional Reading of Genesis One* (Moscow, ID: Canon Press, 1999), 48–49, 62–67; Shaw, "The Literal Day Interpretation," 210–211; D. F. Kelly, *Creation and Change: Genesis 1.1–2.4 in the Light of Changing Scientific Paradigms* (Great Britain: Christian Focus Publications, 1997), 201–207; Sarfati, *Refuting Compromise,* 84–86; Kulikovsky, *A Critique of the Literary Framework View of the Days of Creation,* 7–8; Zylstra, *Revisiting the days of creation. . . again!,* section: "Do these problems really exist?"; McCabe, "A Critique of the Framework Interpretation of the Creation Account (Part 1 of 2)," 43–47; Gentry, "Genesis Creation: Literal or Literary?"

31. Kline, "Because It Had Not Rained," 153; M. Futato, "Because It Had Rained: A Study of Gen. 2:5–7 with Implications for Gen. 2:4–25 and Gen. 1:1–2:3," *Westminster Theological Journal* 60 (1998) 15–17; B. Waltke, "The Literary Genre of Genesis, Chapter One," *Crux* 27:4 (1991) 7; Irons & Kline, "The Framework View," 228–230; Ross, "The Framework Hypothesis," 119–121; Irons, "The Framework Interpretation: An Exegetical Summary," section on the first three days; *The Report of the OPC Committee to study the Framework Hypothesis,* section II, A; Godfrey, *God's Pattern for Creation,* 37–50.

32. *The Report of the OPC Committee to study the Framework Hypothesis,* section II, A; see also Kline, "Space and Time in the Genesis Cosmogony," section "Lower Register Time."

33. Futato, "Because It Had Rained," 16.

34. *Ibid.*, 17.

35. Physicist Russell Humphreys has proposed one possible means of light production in *Starlight and Time* (Green Forest, AR: Master Books, 1994). Physics professor John Hartnett has expanded on this idea in *Starlight, Time and the New Physics* (Powder Springs, GA: Creation Book Publishers, 2007).

36. See Young, "The Days of Genesis" (second article), *Westminster Theological Journal* 25:2 (1963) 153–154.

37. J. Byl, "Testing the Framework Hypothesis: A Response to Dr. W. Robert Godfrey," *Christian Renewal* 19:15 (2001) 14.

38. Godfrey, *God's Pattern for Creation*, 32.

39. *Ibid.*, 42.

40. See Young, "The Days of Genesis," *Westminster Theological Journal* 25:1 (1962) 27–29.

41. Irons & Kline, "The Framework Response," 86.

42. We know almost nothing of the mechanisms of creation. Russell Humphreys has proposed a very interesting mechanism or scenario, which uses principles of special relativity, "white holes" (as opposed to "black holes"), and a time-dilation model to explain one possible series of events. The beauty of the theory is that it is able to account for distant starlight within our approximately six thousand year old universe. See R. Humphreys, *Starlight and Time* (Green Forest, AR: Master Books, 1994). John Hartnett's book also purports to show how light from the most distant stars would have reached earth in a very short time. See J. Hartnett, *Starlight, Time and the*

New Physics (Powder Springs, GA: Creation Book Publishers, 2007).

43. This way of thinking, which imposes our present conditions upon the week of creation, is a recurrent problem in the way the framework proponents understand Genesis 1. The old higher criticism approach seems to have deeply influenced many "conservative" scholars.

44. It is regrettable that the *OCRC Position Paper on Creation* calls all the creation days "six consecutive solar days." According to the literal interpretation, the first three days are precisely *non-solar* days, since they are not governed by the sun.

45. Irons & Kline, "The Framework View," 219.

46. This is the question raised by Irons & Kline, "The Framework View," 229.

47. *The Report of the OPC Committee to study the Framework Hypothesis*, section II, A.

48. Kline, "Space and Time in the Genesis Cosmogony," section "Lower Register Time."

49. Godfrey, *God's Pattern for Creation*, 41.

50. *Ibid.*, 81.

51. *Ibid.*, 81.

52. Ross, "The Framework Hypothesis," 129.

53. The same Hebrew verb "to rule," used in Genesis 1 for the lights, is applied to man in Psalm 8:7.

54. Godfrey, *God's Pattern for Creation*, 41–42.

55. E. J. Young, "The Relation of the First Verse of Genesis One to Verses Two and Three," *Westminster Theological Journal* 21:2 (1959) 141.

56. Iron & Kline, "The Framework View," 230.

57. Carl F. H. Henry has interesting comments on that subject, *God, Revelation and Authority*, vol. 6: *God Who Stands and Stays, Part* 2 (Wheaton, IL: Crossway Books, 1999), 134–136.

58. E. J. Young, *In the Beginning: Genesis Chapters 1 to 3 and the Authority of Scripture* (Edinburg: The Banner of Truth Trust, 1976), 40.

59. J. Calvin, *Commentaries on The First Book of Moses Called Genesis*, vol 1 (Grand Rapids, MI: Baker Books, 2009), 76, emphasis mine.

60. Godfrey, *God's Pattern for Creation*, 81.

61. For a more technical explanation, see R. V. McCabe, "A Defense of Literal Days in the Creation Week," 116–118; McCabe quotes *Genesius' Hebrew Grammar*, 347–348; Paul Joüon, *A Grammar of Biblical Hebrew*, 129–130; *Theological Lexicon of the Old Testament*, 6:14–20; *The Brown-Driver-Briggs Hebrew and English Lexicon*, 400. See also Sarfati, *Refuting Compromise*, 70–71.

62. Genesis 2:4 reads as follows in the Old Latin version: *Hic est liber creaturae caeli et terrae. Cum factus est dies, fecit Deus caelum et terram.* Louis Lavallee, "Augustine on the Creation Days," *Journal of the Evangelical Theological Society* 32:4 (December 1989) 459–460, also available at http://www.etsjets.org/files/JETS-PDFs/32/32-4/32-4-pp457-464_JETS.pdf.

63. For more details on Augustine's view of the days of creation, see Lavallee, "Augustine on the Creation Days," 457–464; Tim Chaffey, "An Examination of Augustine's Commentaries on Genesis One and Their Implications on a Modern Theological Controversy," *Answers Research Journal* 4 (2011) 89-101, also available at http://www.answersingenesis.org/articles/arj/v4/n1/examining-augustine-genesis-commentaries.

64. Godfrey, *God's Pattern for Creation*, 85.

65. *Ibid.*, 90.

66. Jim Witteveen, *God's Pattern for Creation, by W. Robert Godfrey*, available at http://www.jimwitt.ca/?postid=329&replyto=1247563.

67. Godfrey, *God's Pattern for Creation*, 53.

68. *Ibid.*, 85.

69. Kline, "Because It Had Not Rained," 146–157.

70. Blocher, *Révélation des origines*, 47, translation mine.

71. Futato, "Because It Had Rained," *Westminster Theological Journal* 60 (1998) 1–21. See also *The Report of the OPC Committee to study the Framework Hypothesis*, section II, E; Irons & Kline, "The Framework View," 230–236; Ross, "The Framework Hypothesis," 122–128; Irons, "The Framework Interpretation," section on Genesis 2.5; Godfrey, *God's Pattern for Creation*, 52–53. McCabe mentions a number of framework interpreters who do not use Genesis 2:5 to support their interpretation of the literary framework in Genesis 1: V. P. Hamilton, R. K. Hughes, B. K. Waltke and C. J. Fredricks, G. J. Wenham, R. F. Youngblood; see McCabe, "A Critique of

the Framework Interpretation of the Creation Account (Part 2 of 2)," 64.

72. Some arguments presented here have been developed by: Pipa, "From Chaos to Cosmos: A Critique of the Non-Literal Interpretations of Genesis 1:1–2:3," 158–164; Pipa, *From Chaos to Cosmos: A Critique of the Framework Hypothesis*; Jordan, *Creation in Six Days*, 52–57; J. B. Jordan, "Meredith G. Kline Strikes Back (Part 1)," *Biblical Chronology* 9:2 (February 1997); J. B. Jordan, "Meredith G. Kline Strikes Back (Part 2)," *Biblical Chronology* 9:3 (March 1997); Kelly, *Creation and Change*, 121–126; Shaw, "The Literal Day Interpretation," 208–209; Sarfati, *Refuting Compromise*, 98–100; F. Walker, "Genesis One Versus the Framework Hypothesis," *Reformed Herald* 57:6 (February 2001), section on Meredith Kline; F. Walker, "A Critique of the Framework Hypothesis," *Chalcedon Report* 398 (September 1998) 33–34; Zylstra, *Revisiting the days of creation. . . again!*, section "Do these problems really exist?"; *The Days of Creation* (RCUS), section "Framework Theory"; McCabe, "A Critique of the Framework Interpretation of the Creation Account (Part 2 of 2)," 63–108; M. J. Kruger, "An Understanding of Genesis 2:5," *CEN Technical Journal* 11:1 (1997) 106–110; Timothy R. Chaffey, *A Critical Evaluation of the Framework Hypothesis* (Liberty Theological Seminary, 2007), 73–74, also available at http://midwestapologetics.org/articles/theology/frameworkcritique.pdf.

73. Kline, "Because It Had Not Rained," 149–150.

74. See Kline, "Because It Had Not Rained," 148–151; Irons & Kline, "The Framework View," 235–236; Ross, "The Framework Hypothesis," 125–128. Some have rightly criticized the logical fallacy of such an argument, for example: Pipa, "From Chaos to Cosmos: A Critique of the Non-Literal Interpretations of Genesis 1:1–2:3," 162–164.

75. See, for example, Futato, "Because It Had Rained," 5-9.

76. Godfrey, *God's Pattern for Creation*, 81. The rest of our study shows that man was created last and that Genesis 2:5–6 harmonizes very well with the literal reading of Genesis 1. Does Godfrey really believe that man was created before the vegetation? From a long-age point of view, this idea is absurd and rejected by evolutionary theories. From a biblical perspective, if man was created even one day before the vegetation, what would man have eaten during his first day on earth? An earth without trees and fruits and plants is not a habitable place for man (and for animals) to live.

77. Kline, "Because It Had Not Rained," 154.

78. Kruger, "An Understanding of Genesis 2:5," 107.

79. See Young, "The Days of Genesis," 16–23.

80. Kline, "Because It Had Not Rained," 151.

81. *Ibid.*, 151.

82. Kruger, "An Understanding of Genesis 2:5," 109.

83. See Paul Joüon, *Grammaire de l'hébreu biblique* (Rome: Institut Biblique Pontifical, 1923), 283 and 304.

84. A more accurate translation of "La vigueur y a duré pour les faire demeurer en leur nature" would be: "The vigour lasted in them so that they were maintained in their own nature."

85. Calvin, *Commentaries on The First Book of Moses Called Genesis*, 110–111, emphasis mine. See also the annotations to the Dutch Staten Bijbel, as well as Matthew

Henry's commentary, which propose similar explanations.

86. Pipa, "From Chaos to Cosmos: A Critique of the Non-Literal Interpretations of Genesis 1:1–2:3," 161.

87. Kruger, "An Understanding of Genesis 2:5," 109.

88. C. F. Keil, *Commentary on the Old Testament in Ten Volumes, vol. 1: The Pentateuch* (Grand Rapids, MI: Eerdmans, 1986), 77.

89. Kline, "Because It Had Not Rained," 149–150.

90. *Ibid.*, 151.

91. In conclusion of his article "Space and Time in the Genesis Cosmology," 15.

92. Irons & Kline, "The Framework Response," 86.

93. Pipa, "From Chaos to Cosmos: A Critique of the Non-Literal Interpretations of Genesis 1:1–2:3," 163.

94. Kruger, "An Understanding of Genesis 2:5," 108–109.

95. This is what N. H. Ridderbos infers when he questions the nature of the creative act performed on the second day. For him, "the author expresses himself in terms derived from the world-picture of the ancient Orient, or to put it differently, in the terminology current in his day. The ancient Orient generally held to the concept of a celestial arch, which separated the waters above, the heavenly ocean, from the waters beneath." Thus, according to this view, Moses apparently incorporated into the creative account false mythological concepts derived from pagan beliefs. N. H. Ridderbos, *Is There a Conflict Between Genesis 1 And Natural Science?* (Grand

Rapids, MI: Eerdmans, 1957), 43–44. The subject of the alleged "solid dome" will be discussed in more details in the third part of this study.

96. For a presentation of different cosmological views, see Danny Faulkner, *Universe By Design: An Explanation of Cosmology and Creation* (Green Forest, AR: Master Books, 2004).

97. Walker, "Genesis 1 Versus the Framework Hypothesis," 4–5, emphasis mine.

98. Some arguments presented here have been developed by Sarfati, *Refuting Compromise*, 91–93; Pipa, "From Chaos to Cosmos: A Critique of the Non-Literal Interpretations of Genesis 1:1–2:3," 154–157; Pipa, *From Chaos to Cosmos: A Critique of the Framework Hypothesis*.

99. Futato, "Because It Had Rained," 10.

100. Kline, "Because It Had Not Rained," 154; see Irons & Kline, "The Framework View," 221.

101. This grammatical form usually expresses a temporal sequence, but sometimes there are other examples of a *waw* consecutive followed by a verb in the imperfect tense with a pluperfect meaning; see, for example, Exodus 11:1–3 and Numbers 1:47–49.

102. Ross, "The Framework Hypothesis," 124. See also Pipa, "From Chaos to Cosmos: A Critique of the Non-Literal Interpretations of Genesis 1:1–2:3," 156–157.

103. Futato calls the account of Genesis 2 "dis-chronologized" and argues for its topical arrangement, even though it has the grammatical marks of sequential narrative; on this basis, he suggests that Genesis 2 enables us to understand the topical structure of Genesis 1; Futato,

"Because It Had Rained," 10–13. Pipa replies that Futato's argument is contrary to the force of the grammar; there is no compelling evidence to take the second half of Genesis 2 as topical rather than as sequential narrative that uses a pluperfect; Pipa demonstrates that Genesis 2 is primarily chronological narrative; besides, even if Moses arranges a portion of Genesis 2 topically, we still would have no grounds to interpret the first chapter in light of the second; even if Genesis 2 has non-chronological parts, it does not follow that Genesis 1 is non-chronological; Pipa, "From Chaos to Cosmos: A Critique of the Non-Literal Interpretations of Genesis 1:1–2:3," 154–157; Pipa, *From Chaos to Cosmos: A Critique of the Framework Hypothesis*.

104. For example Godfrey, *God's Pattern for Creation*, 67.

105. For a study of the doctrine of creation in church history, see David Hall, *Holding Fast to Creation* (Oak Ridge, TN: The Covenant Foundation, 2001).

106. Ridderbos, *Is There a Conflict Between Genesis 1 And Natural Science?*, 11.

107. Irons & Kline, "The Framework View," 224.

108. Ross, "The Framework Hypothesis," 129.

109. Futato, "Because It Had Rained," 14. Ridderbos had already proposed this pattern, *Is There a Conflict Between Genesis 1 And Natural Science?*, 33.

110. As mentioned previously, the German philosopher Johann Gottfried von Herder (1744–1803) seems to be the father of the theory. The Dutch theologian A. Noordtzij (1924) promoted it. His ideas have been made available in English by N. H. Ridderbos in his book *Is There a Conflict Between Genesis 1 and Natural*

Science? Later on, these ideas have been taken over by many others: Kline, "Because It Had Not Rained," 154; Kline, "Space and Time in the Genesis Cosmogony," see the section on the two registers as well as the tables 1 and 2; Blocher, *Révélation des origines*, 43–51; Irons, "The Framework Interpretation: An Exegetical Summary," second section on the two triads; Futato, "Because It Had Rained," 14–17; Irons & Kline, "The Framework View," 224–230; B. Deffinbaugh, *Genesis: From Paradise to Patriarchs*, Lesson 2: "The Six Days of Creation," available at http://www.bible.ord/series.php?series_id=4; Ward, *Length of Days in Genesis*, sections 2.2 and 2.3; *The Report of the OPC Committee to study the Framework Hypothesis*, section II, B.

111. Some arguments presented here and in the following two sections have been developed by: Young, "The Days of Genesis," 26–31, 153–166; Pipa, "From Chaos to Cosmos: A Critique of the Non-Literal Interpretations of Genesis 1:1–2:3," 172–173; Pipa, *From Chaos to Cosmos: A Critique of the Framework Hypothesis*; Jordan, *Creation in Six Days*, 58–61; W. Grudem, *Systematic Theology: An Introduction to Biblical Doctrine* (Grand Rapids, MI: Zondervan, 1994), 302; Jordan, "Meredith G. Kline Strikes Back (Part 2)"; Sarfati, *Refuting Compromise*, 94–96; Kulikovsky, *A Critique of the Literary Framework View of the Days of Creation*, 9–10; Vincent, *In Defense of God's Creation*, section "Framework Hypothesis"; McCabe, "A Critique of the Framework Interpretation of the Creation Account (Part 1 of 2)," 48–51; Chaffey, *A Critical Evaluation of the Framework Hypothesis*, 60–67.

112. Irons & Kline, "The Framework View," 240; see also Ross, "The Framework Hypothesis," 119.

113. Pipa, "From Chaos to Cosmos: A Critique of the Non-Literal Interpretations of Genesis 1:1–2:3," 188, against

Futato who sees only two "deficiencies"; also Jordan, "Meredith G. Kline Strikes Back (Part 2)," against Kline.

114. Godfrey understands this way the waters in Genesis 1:2, although he does not count four problems but only three, Godfrey, *God's Pattern for Creation*, 38.

115. One informed view in creation based circles holds that the "waters above" refers to waters at the outer edge of the universe. For example, Kurt Wise declares: "The Big-Bang theories include the unboundedness of the universe and its uniform distribution of matter. The universe must have no boundary. Yet Scripture seems to infer that there is a boundary to the universe. On the fourth day of Creation Week, God placed the sun, moon and stars within the firmament (space, or expanse) of the heavens (Genesis 1:14–18). Two days earlier He had placed this firmament in order to separate 'the waters above' from the waters below the expanse (Genesis 1:6–8). There are many different explanations of just what is being referred to by 'the waters above.' When the passage is carefully considered, there is a strong suggestion that all the bodies of the universe are bounded above by 'waters above.' If so, the universe is bounded, and this basic assumption of the Big Bang is invalid." Kurt P. Wise and Sheila A. Richardson, *Something from Nothing: Understanding What You Believe about Creation and Why* (Nashville, TN: Broadman & Holman Publishers, 2004), 52–53. In a footnote the authors refer the reader to D. Faulkner, "The Current State of Creation Astronomy," *Proceedings of the Fourth International Conference on Creationism* (Pittsburgh, PA: Creation Science Fellowship, 1998), 201–216.

116. Irons & Kline, "The Framework View," 228.

117. *Ibid.*, 224. Kline made the same error when he taught on Genesis 1 in his classes, according to C. R. Smith,

one of his students who repeats the same error, see Stephen J. Godfrey & Christopher S. Smith, *Paradigms on Pilgrimage: Creationism, Paleontology, and Biblical Interpretation* (Toronto: Clements, 2005), 111, 137.

118. Irons & Kline, "The Framework View," 228.

119. Ridderbos, *Is There a Conflict Between Genesis 1 And Natural Science?*, 34–35.

120. Futato, "Because It Had Rained," 14.

121. *Ibid.* 14.

122. Irons & Kline, "The Framework View," 228.

123. McCabe, "A Critique of the Framework Interpretation of the Creation Account (Part 1 of 2)," 50.

124. Godfrey, *God's Pattern for Creation*, 25.

125. *Ibid.*, 38.

126. *Ibid.*, 52.

127. *Ibid.*, 25.

128. Godfrey says that the terms "formless and empty" in the Bible describe "an uninhabitable desert" or "a barren waste," *ibid.*, 25; this is a good description of the situation after God gathered the waters into one place and before He created the plants; the dry land was dry, but still empty.

129. *Ibid.*, 81.

130. *Ibid.*, 56–57.

131. According to Godfrey, "the days are actual for us but figurative for God," "these ordinary days are for us as a model for our working, not as a time schedule that God followed," *ibid.*, 90.

132. Jordan, *Creation in Six Days*, 211–226.

133. Andrew Kulikovsky has reviewed Jordan's book and has criticized his approach, A. Kulikovsky, "The Right Conclusion from the Wrong Interpretation," *Technical Journal* 19:2 (2005) 64–66, also available at http://creation.com/images/pdfs/tj/j19_2/j19_2_64-66.pdf.

134. Young, "The Days of Genesis" (second article), 152, emphasis mine.

135. Young, "The Days of Genesis," 23–24.

136. Blocher, *In the Beginning: The Opening Chapters of Genesis*, 50–51.

137. *Ibid.*, 53.

138. The original French "*prose plate*" is more negative than "two-dimensional prose."

139. J.-M. Berthoud, "Débat public sur la doctrine biblique de la création," *Positions créationnistes* 12 (May1990) 7, translation mine; also available at http://calvinisme.ch/index.php/BERTHOUD_Jean-Marc_-_Henri_BLOCHER_-_D%C3%A9bat_public_sur_la_doctrine_biblique_de_la_cr%C3%A9ation. See also Young, "The Days of Genesis," 16, 23–24.

140. Kelly, *Creation and Change*, 115. For other arguments in favour of the idea that the literary and historical aspects are not mutually exclusive, see K. L. Gentry, "In

the Space of Six Days," *Ordained Servant* 9:1 (January 2000), 4th objection.

141. J. MacArthur, Genesis 1: Fact or Framework?, available at http://www.gty.org/Resources/Articles/2422. MacArthur's perspicacity is proven true. Blocher, in his *Révélation des origines,* does not stop his figurative reading at the end of the creation week. He also sees several figurative elements in Genesis 2–3: the two trees (120–121); Eve's creation from Adam's rib (93–94); the serpent (177); and possibly the four rivers (152). Blocher says (my translation): "The real problem is not to know if we have a historical account (historian) of the fall, but if we have an account of a historical fall" (152). What does that mean? Blocher explains this subtle but important distinction by comparing Genesis 3 with the two accounts of the same historical sin of David in 2 Samuel 11 and 12. Nathan's parable is as historical as the factual account of the events preceding it. This parable is about David's real, historical sin. Nathan cannot be accused of having told a myth or a legend. He relates a real, historical fact in the figure of a parable. This implies that, for Blocher, the account of the fall in Genesis 3 might as well be a parable, in which the factual elements are not necessarily historical, but the account still conveys the historical sin of Adam and Eve. Moses has imaginatively reconstructed the initial event, which does not mean that the historicity is insignificant for his purposes. In a word, for Blocher, Genesis 3 is a complete reconstruction of the facts, as much as Nathan's parable was a reconstruction of what really happened. The problem is that we know what happened in David's life because we have a previous factual account, but we don't know what happened to Adam and Eve if we are left with only a parable. Why would Moses have used such a parable of the fall, if not to confuse the reader? He pretends the account is factual, but actually deceives the reader, who is left to

imagine what actually happened. With such a figurative reading, Genesis 3 is open to interpretation. And the speculation begins. Perhaps Adam and Eve never existed (as the poor, the rich, and the flocks in Nathan's parable never really existed). Perhaps they are figures symbolizing our present condition. Tim Keller, who has read Blocher, also believes that the first chapters of Genesis contain several figurative elements. He concludes: "It looks like a responsible way of reading the text is to interpret Genesis 2–3 as the account of an historical event that really happened" (*Creation, Evolution, and Christian Laypeople, 8*). Readers will need to discern what Keller is saying here and not be fooled by the language. Keller's "account of an historical event" is very similar to Blocher's "account of a historical fall," as opposed to "a historical account of the fall." MacArthur is right. When one begins to read Genesis 1 figuratively, there is no telling where one will stop.

142. Marc Kay, "On literary theorists' approach to Genesis 1: Part 1," 71.

143. *Ibid.*, 72.

144. Marc Kay, "On literary theorists' approach to Genesis 1: Part 2," *Journal of Creation* 21:3 (2007) 97, also available at http://creation.com/images/pdfs/tj/j21_3/j21_3_93-101.pdf.

145. McCabe, "A Critique of the Framework Interpretation of the Creation Account (Part 1 of 2)," 35; for a more detailed analysis of the use of the *waw* consecutive in the creation account, see 57–65.

146. *Ibid.*, 34. McCabe compares Genesis 1:1–2:3 with Job 38:8–11, Ps. 33:6–9, and Ps. 104:5–9, three texts presenting some details from the creation week, which exhibit a consistent use of linear parallelism.

147. Pipa, "From Chaos to Cosmos: A Critique of the Non-Literal Interpretations of Genesis 1:1–2:3," 189.

148. Grudem, *Systematic Theology*, 303.

149. Godfrey, *God's Pattern for Creation*, 93.

150. *Ibid.*, 25.

151. *Ibid.*, 32.

152. *Ibid.*, 35.

153. *Ibid.*, 48–49.

154. *Ibid.*, 51.

155. *Ibid.*, 73.

156. *Ibid.*, 89.

157. *Ibid.*, 53.

158. Young, "The Days of Genesis" (second article), 166.

159. *Ibid.*, 153–166; see also Pipa, "From Chaos to Cosmos: A Critique of the Non-Literal Interpretations of Genesis 1:1–2:3," 189; Kulikovsky, *A Critique of the Literary Framework View of the Days of Creation*, 16–17; Kelly, *Creation and Change*, 206.

160. Godfrey, *God's Pattern for Creation*, 22.

161. *Ibid.*, 31–32.

162. *Ibid.*, 71.

163. *Ibid.*, 80–81.

164. *Ibid.*, 85.

165. *Ibid.*, 86.

166. Jim Witteveen, *God's Pattern for Creation, by W. Robert Godfrey*.

167. *Idem.*

168. Irons & Kline, "The Framework View," 184.

169. Godfrey, *God's Pattern for Creation*, 85.

170. Blocher, *In the Beginning: The Opening Chapters of Genesis*, 53.

171. Godfrey, *God's Pattern for Creation*, 90.

172. Ross, "The Framework Hypothesis: An Interpretation of Genesis 1:1–2:3," 128.

173. *The Report of the OPC Committee to Study the Framework Hypothesis*, Section C on "The Eternal Nature of the Seventh Day."

174. Irons & Kline, "The Framework View," 245.

175. *Ibid.*, 219.

176. Ross, "The Framework Hypothesis: An Interpretation of Genesis 1:1–2:3," 122.

177. Godfrey, *God's Pattern for Creation*, 90.

178. *Ibid.* 90.

179. L. Berkhof, *Systematic Theology* (Grand Rapids, MI: Eerdmans, 1939, 1941), 153.

180. For example see Waltke, "The Literary Genre of Genesis, Chapter One"; Ward, *Length of Days in Genesis*, section 2.1; Futato, "Because It Had Rained," 18–21. Others have refuted their arguments, for example: Jordan, *Creation in Six Days*, 34–39, 235–245; Sarfati, *Refuting Compromise*, 96–98.

181. Godfrey, *God's Pattern for Creation*, 18.

182. Futato, "Because It Had Rained," 20.

183. This is the opinion of Deffinbaugh, who believes in the framework theory, *Genesis: From Paradise to Patriarchs*, Lesson 2, "The Historical Backdrop of Genesis 1" and "The Meaning of Creation for the Israelites of Old."

184. F. Walker makes this point and shows that the idea of a polemic against Baal worship does not come from the text but from outside of the text. He correctly adds that M. Futato's approach is an adaptation of the critical methods of the liberal theologians. Walker, "Genesis 1 Versus the Framework Hypothesis," section on Mark D. Futato.

185. See Young, "The Days of Genesis" (second article), 148–149; D. Batten & J. Sarfati, in *15 Reasons to Take Genesis as History* (Brisbane: Creation Ministries International, 2006), 8–10, highlight the fact that the first two chapters of Genesis are an integral part of a historical book.

186. For a semantic approach to the days of creation, see the detailed study done by J. Stambaugh, who concludes unequivocally that in Genesis 1 God could not have communicated more clearly that the days of creation are literal. The studies done by G. F. Hasel, K. L. Gentry, and R. V. McCabe come to the same conclusion (see the bibliography).

187. Peter J. Wallace, *Evening and Morning*, available at http://www.peterwallace.org/essays/evening.htm. The other quotations in the same paragraph and in the next come from the same source.

188. See, for example, Kelly, *Creation and Change*, 129–134; Batten & Sarfati, *15 Reasons to Take Genesis as History*, 11–19.

189. See, for example, Pipa, "From Chaos to Cosmos: A Critique of the Non-Literal Interpretations of Genesis 1:1–2:3," 168–171; R. V. McCabe, "A Critique of the Framework Interpretation of the Creation Account (Part 2 of 2)," 108–117.

190. Noel Weeks, *The Sufficiency of Scripture* (Edinburg: The Banner of Truth Trust, 1988), 108, quoted by Pipa, "From Chaos to Cosmos: A Critique of the Non-Literal Interpretations of Genesis 1:1–2:3," 170.

191. Godfrey, *God's Pattern for Creation*, 96.

192. *Ibid.*, 62; see also Godfrey, "Genesis One and the Church Today," *Christian Renewal* 19:9 (January 29, 2001) 12–13.

193. See Young, "The Days of Genesis" (second article), 143–147; Pipa, "From Chaos to Cosmos: A Critique of the Non-Literal Interpretations of Genesis 1:1–2:3," 169–171; Walker, "Genesis One Versus the Framework Hypothesis," section on the fourth commandment. For Young, Pipa, Walker, and many others, the fourth commandment is a decisive argument against a non-chronological understanding of the six days of creation.

194. Noel Weeks, "The Hermeneutical Problem of Genesis 1–11," *Themelios* 4:1 (September 1978) 18.

195. See R. J. Vincent, *In Defense of God's Creation: A Personal Position Paper*, section on the first day, available at http://www.theocentric.com/originalarticles/creation.html.

196. Godfrey, *God's Pattern for Creation*, 43–44.

197. François du Toit tells this interesting anecdote: "I read an article in a business publication that described our existence using the billion-year evolutionary worldview. It put the whole evolutionary process into one year as an analogy. The big bang was on 1 January and we're now at midnight 31 December. The Milky Way came into existence in March, the first cell in August and the first vertebrates on December 17. Humans appeared on December 31 at 11:54 pm and recorded history only covers the last 10 seconds. I'm glad the Bible reveals the truth that we are the crown of God's creation. Although humans are but a small speck in the (young) universe we are important enough for the Father to love us and give His Son to stand in our place and be judged for our sins." *Creation* 33:1 (2011) 5.

198. R. V. McCabe, "A Critique of the Framework Interpretation of the Creation Week," *Coming to Grips with Genesis: Biblical Authority and the Age of the Earth* (Green Forest, AR: Master Books, 2008) 249.

199. Some arguments presented here have been developed by Jordan, *Creation in Six Days*, 71–87; J. B. Jordan, "The Framework Hypothesis," *Biblical Chronology* 3:6 (June 1991).

200. Kim Riddlebarger, R. Scott Clark, and Michael Scott Horton, "Slippery Slope or No Slope?" *Christian Renewal* 19:10 (February 26, 2001) 4.

201. *The Report of the OPC Committee to study the Framework Hypothesis*, section II, A.

202. Jordan, *Creation in Six Days*, 71–87.

203. Stephen J. Godfrey & Christopher R. Smith, *Paradigms on Pilgrimage: Creationism, Paleontology, and Biblical Interpretation*, Part 2: Creationism and Biblical Interpretation (Toronto: Clements, 2005), 93–207.

204. *Ibid.*, 106.

205. *Ibid.*, 111.

206. *Ibid.*, 115.

207. *Ibid.*, 125.

208. *Ibid.*, 126.

209. *Ibid.*, 128.

210. Andrew Kulikovsky, "The Right Conclusion from the Wrong Interpretation," *Technical Journal* 19:2 (2005) 64.

211. Kim Riddlebarger, R. Scott Clark, and Michael Scott Horton, "Slippery Slope or No Slope?" 4.

212. Godfrey & Smith, *Paradigms on Pilgrimage: Creationism, Paleontology, and Biblical Interpretation*, 141.

213. *Ibid.*, 137.

214. *Ibid.*, 151.

215. *Ibid.*, 190.

216. Ridderbos, *Is There a Conflict Between Genesis 1 And Natural Science?*, 43–44.

217. Kline, "Because It Had Not Rained," 149–150.

218. Futato, "Because It Had Rained," 17.

219. Blocher, *In the Beginning: The Opening Chapters of Genesis*, 53.

220. Weeks, "The Hermeneutical Problem of Genesis 1–11," 18.

221. Futato, "Because It Had Rained," 20.

222. Godfrey, *God's Pattern for Creation*, 31.

223. Godfrey & Smith, *Paradigms on Pilgrimage: Creationism, Paleontology, and Biblical Interpretation*, 196.

224. *Ibid.*, 192.

225. *Ibid.*, 135.

226. *Ibid.*, 182–183.

227. Faulkner, *Universe by Design*, 96. Used with permission from the publisher Master Books.

228. *Ibid.*, 109–110. Used with permission from the publisher Master Books.

229. Pipa, *From Chaos to Cosmos: A Critique of the Framework Hypothesis*, in his introduction.

230. Calvin, *Commentaries on The First Book of Moses Called Genesis*, 78, emphasis mine.

231. Godfrey, *God's Pattern for Creation*, 98, emphasis mine.

232. *Ibid.*, 99, emphasis mine.

233. *Ibid.*, 62, emphasis mine.

234. *Ibid.*, 105, emphasis mine.

235. *Ibid.*, 105. Remember that according to Godfrey and contrary to Calvin, "the days are actual for us but figurative for God; they are not a timetable of God's actions but are a model timetable for us to follow," *ibid.*, 90.

236. Jim Witteveen, *God's Pattern for Creation, by W. Robert Godfrey*. See also John Byl, *Accommodating Error*, available at http://bylogos.blogspot.com/2010/03/accommodating-error.html.

237. *The Report of the OPC Committee to study the Framework Hypothesis*, section II, C.

238. Kline, "Space and time in the Genesis Cosmogony"; Irons & Kline, "The Framework View," 236–248; Irons, "The Framework Interpretation: An Exegetical Summary," section on the seventh day.

239. Pipa, "From Chaos to Cosmos: A Critique of the Non-Literal Interpretations of Genesis 1:1–2:3," 184.

240. Some arguments presented here have been developed by Jordan, *Creation in Six Days*, 67–68, 87–90; Jordan, "Meredith G. Kline Strikes Back (Part 2)"; Kulikovsky, *A Critique of the Literary Framework View of the Days of Creation*, 11; Walker, "Genesis 1 Versus the Framework Hypothesis," section entitled "Meredith G. Kline, 'Space and Time'"; McCabe, "A Critique of the Framework Interpretation of the Creation Account (Part 2 of

2)," 117–131; Chaffey, *A Critical Evaluation of the Framework Hypothesis*, 75–78.

241. Walker, "Genesis 1 Versus the Framework Hypothesis," section on Kline, "Space and Time."

242. Godfrey, *God's Pattern for Creation*, 53.

243. McCabe, "A Critique of the Framework Interpretation of the Creation Account (Part 2 of 2)," 128.

244. Jordan, *Creation in Six Days*, 62.

245. *Ibid.*, 62–63. For other critics of Kline's "two-register cosmology," see Pipa, "From Chaos to Cosmos: A Critique of the Non-Literal Interpretations of Genesis 1:1–2:3," 192–193; Jordan, "Meredith G. Kline Strikes Back (Part 2)"; McCabe, "A Critique of the Framework Interpretation of the Creation Account (Part 2 of 2),"117–131; Chaffey, *A Critical Evaluation of the Framework Hypothesis*, 75–78.

246. For example, see L. Irons and M. Kline, "The Framework Reply," *The Genesis Debate: Three Views on the Days of Creation* (Mission Viejo, CA: Crux Press, 2001), 279–292, who answer this way to the critics presented by J. Ligon Duncan III and David W. Hall, "The 24-Hour Response" [to the Framework View], *The Genesis Debate: Three Views on the Days of Creation* (Mission Viejo, CA: Crux Press, 2001), 257–268.

247. One example among others is the idea that the framework interpretation maintains that God created everything by natural providence, which is a false representation of this view; see L. F. DeBoer, *The Framework Hypothesis*, who makes this mistake, available at http://www.americanpresbyterianchurch.org/?page_id=136.

248. Chaffey, *A Critical Evaluation of the Framework Hypothesis*, 83.

249. *Report of the Creation Study Committee* (PCA), section IV, C, objection 6, available at http://www.pcahistory.org/creation/report.html.

250. Herman Hanko, *The Framework Hypothesis and Genesis 1*, available at http://www.prca.org/pamphlets/pamphlet_83.html. Hanko expresses deep concern about the framework hypothesis and concludes that this very complex interpretation is an assault on the simplicity, the perspicuity, and the authority of the Scriptures.

251. J. C. VanDyken, "The Framework Hypothesis," *The Trumpet* 12:4 (April 2000) 8.

252. Chaffey, *A Critical Evaluation of the Framework Hypothesis*, 81.

253. Godfrey, *God's Pattern for Creation*, 14.

254. This is also the opinion of Frank Walker, who considers the framework approach as attacking the clarity of Scripture; Walker, "A Critique of the Framework Hypothesis," 32. J. C. VanDyken has the same concern with the framework interpretation and asserts that Genesis is crystal clear; "The Framework Hypothesis," *The Trumpet* 12:2 (Feb. 2000) 7–9, and 12:5 (May 2000) 9–10.

255. Many people come to that conclusion, for example: Kulikovsky, *A Critique of the Literary Framework View of the Days of Creation*, 17; Stambaugh, "The Days of Creation: A Semantic Approach," conclusion.

256. Sarfati, *Refuting Compromise*, 105, in the conclusion of his excellent chapter on the days of creation.

257. This is the opinion of R. Grigg, "How Long Were the Days of Creation?," who also concludes that God could not have more clearly expressed the fact that He created the world during a period of six days of a normal duration.

258. This is the concern expressed by M. Zylstra, *Revisiting the days of creation. . . again!*, section "Hermeneutic of the Doctrine of Creation."

259. See also Byl, "Testing the Framework Hypothesis: A Response to Dr. W. Robert Godfrey," 14; Jordan, "Meredith G. Kline Strikes Back (Part 1)"; J. C. VanDyken, "The Framework Hypothesis," *The Trumpet* 12:6 (June 2000) 8–11.

260. Blocher, *In the Beginning: The Opening Chapters of Genesis*, 48.

261. *Ibid.*, 50.

262. Kline, "Because It Had Not Rained," 157.

263. Kline, "Space and Time in the Genesis Cosmogony," 2.

264. Chaffey, *A Critical Evaluation of the Framework Hypothesis*, 83.

265. Kline, "Space and Time in the Genesis Cosmogony," note 47 in his conclusion.

266. VanDyken, "The Framework Hypothesis," *The Trumpet* 12:6 (June 2000) 10.

267. Byl, "Testing the Framework Hypothesis: A Response to Dr. W. Robert Godfrey," 14; the quotes are from Godfrey, "Genesis One and the Church Today," 12.

268. Godfrey, *God's Pattern for Creation*, 91.

269. Dr. Don Batten (plant physiology, agricultural science, Ph.D. from the University of Sidney); Dr. Jerry Bergman (biology, biochemistry, pathology, Ph.D. from Columbia Pacific University); Dr. John Byl (astronomy, physics, mathematics, Ph.D. from the University of British Columbia); Dr. Danny Faulkner (cosmology, astrophysics, Ph.D. from Indiana University); Dr. John Hartnett (physics, cosmology, Ph.D. from the University of Western Australia); Dr. Russell Humphreys (physics, Ph.D. from Louisiana State University); Dr. Jonathan Sarfati (physical chemistry, Ph.D. from Victoria University of Wellington, New Zealand, former New Zealand Chess Champion and F.I.D.E. Master); Dr. Kurt Wise (geology, Ph.D. from Harvard University, under the supervision of Stephen Jay Gould).

270. If Ben Stein's 2008 documentary film *Expelled: No Intelligence Allowed* was the tip, then Dr. Jerry Bergman's book is the rest of the iceberg. Jerry Bergman, *Slaughter of the Dissidents. The Shocking Truth About Killing the Careers of Darwin Doubters* (Southworth, WA: Leafcutter Press, 2008). This extended book (480 pages) is the first of a projected three volume set. Christian persecution in academia is widespread, destroying countless careers and families today. In real life cases, Dr. Bergman documents the strategies anti-Christians use to suppress intellectual freedom in our universities. No matter how promising the career, no matter how impressive the publications, and no matter how significant the research, a failure to abide by Darwinism is a career killer in almost any academic field. Many scientists, simply because they question the orthodoxy of neo-Darwinism, are losing their jobs, cannot get tenure, are denied publication in scientific journals, and are openly ridiculed and ostracized by their peers.

271. Several organizations produce a lot of materials and make available a tremendous amount of in-depth researches and relevant information, for example: Creation Ministries International (creation.com), Answers in Genesis (www.answersingenesis.org), The Institute for Creation Research (www.icr.org). The CMI website also gives a long list of many other helpful Christian ministries and websites dedicated to the same cause.

272. Todd S. Beall, *Christians in the Public Square: How Far Should Evangelicals Go in the Creation-Evolution Debate?*, 2006, 5–6, available at www.biblearchaeology.org/file.axd?file=Creation+Evolution+Debate+Beall.pdf.

273. J. MacArthur, *Genesis 1: Fact or Framework?*, available at http://www.gty.org/Resources/Articles/2422.

274. Tremper Longman III, *How to Read Genesis* (Downers Grove, IL: InterVarsity Press, 2005), 104.

275. *Ibid.*, 104.

276. Bruce Waltke, *Barriers to Accepting the Possibility of Creation by Means of an Evolutionary Process*, 9, available at www.biologos.org/uploads/projects/Waltke_scholarly_essay.pdf.

277. H. Van Till, *The Fourth Day: What the Bible and the Heavens Are Telling Us About Creation* (Grand Rapids, MI: Eerdmans, 1986), 84–85.

278. H. Van Till, "The Fully Gifted Creation," *Three Views on Creation and Evolution*, Grand Rapids, MI: Zondervan, 1999, ed. J. P. Moreland & J. M. Reynolds. For a critique of this book, see Andrew Kulikovsky, "A balanced

treatment?? A Review of 'Three views on creation and evolution,'" *CEN Technical Journal* 14:1 (2000) 23–27, also available at http://creation.com/images/pdfs/tj/j14_1/j14_1_23-27.pdf.

279. See John Van Dyk, "Fourth Day author aboard process theology train," *Christian Renewal* 23:16 (2005) 14–15, 17.

280. See John Byl, "The Evolution of Calvin College," *Christian Renewal* 29:5 (2010) 6–8.

281. J. A. Thompson, "Genesis 1: Science? History? Theology?," *Theological Students Fellowship Bulletin 50* (Spring 1968) 20.

282. Tim Keller, *Creation, Evolution, and Christian Laypeople,* available at http://www.biologos.org/uploads/projects/Keller_white_paper.pdf, 13.

283. *Ibid.*, 4. In his footnotes, Keller refers to the works of Blocher and Kline on Genesis 1–2, thus showing his association with the framework proponents, although he gets somewhat confused with some aspects of the framework view. For a refutation of Keller's paper, see John Byl, *Genesis vs Dr. Tim Keller*, available at http://bylogos.blogspot.com/2010/02/genesis-versus-dr-tim-keller.html. See also Lita Cosner, *A Response to Timothy Keller's "Creation, Evolution, and Christian Laypeople,"* available at http://creation.com/timothy-keller-response. Byl points out that "on Keller's own reading of Gen. 2:5, there are *two* reasons for lack of vegetation: no rain and no man. This entails that Adam was created *before* vegetation. . . Yet this, if anything, makes things much worse for anyone trying to reconcile Genesis with evolution." For a review of Keller's book *The Reason for God, Belief in an Age of Skepticism*

(New York, NY: Dutton, 2008), where his views of creation, sin and suffering are warped by his theistic evolutionary beliefs, see Lita Cosner, *Apologetic Against Atheism Flawed by theistic Evolutionary Stance*, available at http://creation.com/review-timothy-keller-reason-for-god. According to BioLogos, Keller's book "focuses especially on the interaction of science and religion, maintaining that evolutionary theory need not be considered a deathblow to faith," available at http://biologos.org/resources/timothy-keller.

284. Available at http://www.biologos.org/projects/workshops.

285. Darrel Falk, *On Coming to Peace in the Family of God*, available at http://www.biologos.org/projects/workshops.

286. Lydia Jaeger, *Baptiser Darwin? Le pasteur et la théorie de l'évolution*, 1, my translation, available at http://ljaeger.ibnogent.org/uploads/articles/Le%20Pasteur%20et%20%20Evolution.pdf.

287. See their website at http://rescev.free.fr.

288. Several books and articles have shown that embracing the theory of evolution is absolutely not an option for Christians, first and foremost for biblical reasons but also for scientific reasons. For example, see Norman C. Nevin, ed., *Should Christians Embrace Evolution? Biblical and Scientific Responses* (Nottingham, UK: Intervarsity Press, 2009). In his review of this book, Dr. Cornelis Van Dam summarizes the cost of theistic evolution: "As this book explains, to accept theistic evolution means denying the biblical doctrines of the unity of the human race, the uniqueness of human beings, the special creation of Adam and Eve in the image of God, the

goodness of God's original creation, and the teaching that death and suffering are the result of sin. Furthermore, since theistic evolution postulates pre-Adamite humans and the reality of human death before Adam and Eve, one can no longer assert with Scripture that as sin entered the world through one man, and death through sin, so the new creation and life comes through the second Adam Jesus Christ (Rom 5:12–21). To accept evolution as a model to explain Genesis 1 means denying what Scripture says about creation, fall, and redemption. The Darwinian evolutionary worldview and the biblical one stand opposed to each other." C. Van Dam, "Should We Accept Evolution?," *Clarion* 60:3 (January 28, 2011) 57. See also Jonathan Sarfati's books, *Refuting Evolution* (Green Forest, AR: Master Books, 1999); *Refuting Evolution 2* (Green Forest, AR: Master Books, 2002); *Refuting Compromise: A Biblical and Scientific Refutation of "Progressive Creationism" (Billions of Years), As Popularized by Astronomer Hugh Ross* (Green Forest, AR: Master Books, 2004).

289. Weeks, "The Hermeneutical Problem of Genesis 1–11," 19.

290. Chaffey, *A Critical Evaluation of the Framework Hypothesis*, 53.

BIBLIOGRAPHY

In favour of the framework interpretation:

The Report of the OPC Committee to study the Framework Hypothesis. Presented at the Presbytery of Southern California (OPC) during its meeting on October 15–16, 1999. Available at http://www.asa3.org/gray/framework/frameworkOPC-SC.html.

Blocher, Henri. *Révélation des origines*. Lausanne: Presses Bibliques Universitaires, 1979.

______. *In the Beginning: The Opening Chapters of Genesis.* Translated by David G. Preston. Downers Grove, IL: InterVarsity Press, 1984.

Deffinbaugh, Bob. *Genesis: From Paradise to Patriarchs.* Available at http://www.bible.org/series.php?series_id=4.

Futato, Mark D. "Because It Had Rained: A Study of Gen 2:5–7 with Implications for Gen 2:4–25 and Gen 1:1–2:3." *Westminster Theological Journal* 60 (1998) 1–21. Also available at http://faculty.gordon.edu/hu/bi/Ted_Hildebrandt/OTeSources/01-Genesis/Text/Articles-Books/Futato_RainGen2_WTJ.pdf.

Godfrey, Stephen J., and Christopher R. Smith. *Paradigms on Pilgrimage. Creationism, Paleontology, and Biblical Interpretation.* Toronto: Clements, 2005.

Godfrey, W. Robert. "Genesis One and the Church Today," *Christian Renewal* 19:9 (January 29, 2001) 12–13.

_______. *God's Pattern for Creation.* Phillipsburg, NJ: Presbyterian & Reformed, 2003.

Hagopian, David G., ed. *The Genesis Debate: Three Views on the Days of Creation.* Mission Viejo, CA: Crux Press, 2001.

- Lee Irons and Meredith G. Kline wrote the sections in favour of the framework interpretation:
  "The Framework Response" [to the 24-Hour View], 83–95.
  "The Framework Response" [to the Day-Age View], 179–188.
  "The Framework View," 217–256.
  "The Framework Reply," 279–303.

- J. Ligon Duncan III and David W. Hall (in favour of the 24-Hour view) wrote a response:
  "The 24-Hour Response" [to the Framework View], 257–268.

- Hugh Ross and Gleason L. Archer (in favour of the Day-Age view) wrote a response:
  "The Day-Age Response" [to the Framework View], 269–277.

- The book has been reviewed by Scott Yoshikawa:
  http://www.upper-register.com/papers/review_genesis_debate.html.

Hamilton, Victor P. *The Book of Genesis: Chapters 1–17*. New International Commentary on the Old Testament. Grand Rapids, MI: Eerdmans, 1990.

Hughes, R. Kent. *Genesis: Beginning and Blessing*. Preaching the Word. Wheaton, IL: Crossway Books, 2004.

Irons, Lee. "The Framework Interpretation: An Exegetical Summary." *Ordained Servant* 9:1 (January 2000) 7–11. Also available at http://opc.org/OS/pdf/OSV9N1.pdf.

Jaeger, Lydia. *Baptiser Darwin? Le pasteur et la théorie de l'évolution*. Available at http://ljaeger.ibnogent.org/uploads/articles/Le%20Pasteur%20et%20%20Evolution.pdf.

Keller, Tim. *Creation, Evolution, and Christian Laypeople*. Available at http://www.biologos.org/uploads/projects/Keller_white_paper.pdf.

Kline, Meredith G. "Because It Had Not Rained." *Westminster Theological Journal* 20:2 (May 1958) 146–157. Also available at http://www.asa3.org/ASA/resources/WTJ/WTJ58Kline.html.

———. "Space and Time in the Genesis Cosmogony." *Perspectives on Science and Christian Faith* 48:1 (March 1996) 2–15. Also available at http://www.asa3.org/ASA/PSCF/1996/PSCF3-96Kline.html.

Ramm, Bernard. *The Christian View of Science and Scripture*. Grand Rapids, MI: Eerdmans, 1954.

Ridderbos, N. H. *Is There a Conflict Between Genesis 1 and Natural Science?* Grand Rapids, MI: Eerdmans, 1957.

Ross, Mark. "The Framework Hypothesis: An Interpretation of Genesis 1:1–2:3." In *Did God Create in Six Days?* ed. Joseph A. Pipa & David W. Hall, 113–130. Greenville, SC: Southern Presbyterian Press, 1999.

Throntveit, Mark A. "Are the Events in the Genesis Creation Account Set Forth in Chronological Order? No." In *The Genesis Debate: Persistent Questions about Creation and the Flood,* ed. Ronald Youngblood, 36–55. Nashville, TN: Thomas Nelson, 1986.

Van Till, Howard. H. *The Fourth Day: What the Bible and the Heavens Are Telling Us About Creation*. Grand Rapids, MI: Eerdmans, 1986.

Waltke, Bruce K. "The Literary Genre of Genesis, Chapter One. *Crux* 27:4 (1991) 2–10.

Waltke, Bruce K., and Cathi J. Fredricks. *Genesis: A Commentary*. Grand Rapids, MI: Zondervan, 2001.

Ward, Rowland S. *Length of Days in Genesis*. Available at http://www.spindleworks.com/library/ward/framework.htm.

Wenham, Gordon J. *Genesis 1–15.* Word Biblical Commentary. Nashville, TN: Thomas Nelson, 1987.

Youngblood, Ronald F. *The Book of Genesis.* 2nd ed. Grand Rapids, MI: Baker, 1991.

Against the framework interpretation:

Batten, Don, ed. *The Creation Answers Book*. Chapter 2: "Six Days? Really?" Powder Springs, GA: Creation Book Publishers, 2007. Also available at http://www.creationontheweb.com/images/pdfs/cabook/chapter2.pdf.

Batten, D., D. Catchpoole, J. Sarfati, and C. Wieland. *Is Genesis poetry/figurative, a theological argument (polemic) and thus not history? Critique of the Framework Hypothesis*. Also available at http://creation.com/is-genesis-poetry-figurative-a-theological-argument-polemic-and-thus-not-history.

Beall, Todd S. *Christians in the Public Square: How Far Should Evangelicals Go in the Creation-Evolution Debate?* 2006. Available at www.biblearchaeology.org/file.axd?file=Creation+Evolution+Debate+Beall.pdf.

Berthoud, Jean-Marc, and Serge Rambert. "Révélation des origines: Une réponse." *Position créationnistes* 11 (February 1990).

Byl, John. *Accommodating Error*. Available at http://bylogos.blogspot.com/2010/03/accommodating-error.html.

_______. "Testing the Framework Hypothesis: A Response to Dr. W. Robert Godfrey." *Christian Renewal* 19:15 (April 30, 2001) 14–15.

_______. "The Evolution of Calvin College." *Christian Renewal* 29:5 (2010) 6–8.

_______. *Genesis vs Dr. Tim Keller*. Available at http://bylogos.blogspot.com/2010/02/genesis-versus-dr-tim-keller.html.

Chaffey, Timothy R. *A Critical Evaluation of the Framework Hypothesis*. Liberty Theological Seminary, 2007. Also available at http://midwestapologetics.org/articles/theology/frameworkcritique.pdf.

Cosner, Lita. *A Response to Timothy Keller's "Creation, Evolution, and Christian Laypeople."* Available at http://creation.com/timothy-keller-response.

Courthial, P., P. Berthoud, H. Blocher, and J.-M. Berthoud. "Débat public sur la doctrine biblique de la création." *Positions créationnistes* 12 (May 1990). Also available at http://calvinisme.ch/index.php/BERTHOUD_Jean-Marc_-_Henri_BLOCHER_-_D%C3%A9bat_public_sur_la_doctrine_biblique_de_la_cr%C3%A9ation.

DeBoer, Louis F. *The Framework Hypothesis*. Available at http://www.americanpresbyterianchurch.org/?page_id=136.

Engelsma, David J. *Genesis 1–11: Myth or History?* Available at http://www.mountainretreatorg.net/apologetics/genesis111.html.

Gentry, Kenneth L., Jr. "Genesis Creation: Literal or Literary?" *Chalcedon Report* 452 (May 2003). Also available at http://www.banneroftruth.org/pages/articles/article_detail.php?473.

_______. "In the Space of Six Days." *Ordained Servant* 9:1 (January 2000) 12–16. Also available at http://opc.org/OS/html/V9/1d.html.

_______. "Reformed Theology and Six-Day Creation." *Chalcedon Report* 398 (September 1998) 26–29. Also available at http://www.the-highway.com/creation_Gentry.html.

Gentry, K. L., Jr., and M. Butler. *Yea, Hath God Said? The Framework Hypothesis/Six-Day Creation Debate*. Eugene, OR: Wipf & Stock, 2002.

Reviewed by Andrew Kulikovsky. "The Keys to Interpreting Genesis: History and Genre." *Technical Journal* 18:3 (2004) 61–62. Also available at http://creation.com/images/pdfs/tj/j18_3/j18_3_61-62.pdf.

Hanko, Herman. *The Framework Hypothesis and Genesis 1*. Available at http://www.prca.org/pamphlets/pamphlet_83.html.

Hasel, Gerhard F. "The 'Days' of Creation in Genesis 1: Literal 'Days' or Figurative 'Periods/Epochs' of Time?" *Origins* 21:1 (1994) 5–37.

Jordan, James B. *Creation in Six Days: A Defense of the Traditional Reading of Genesis One*. Moscow, ID: Canon Press, 1999.

_______. "Meredith G. Kline Strikes Back (Part 1)." *Biblical Chronology* 9:2 (February 1997). Also available at http://reformed-theology.org/ice/newslet/bc/bc.97.02.htm.

_______. "Meredith G. Kline Strikes Back (Part 2)." *Biblical Chronology* 9:3 (March 1997). Also available at http://reformed-theology.org/ice/newslet/bc/bc.97.03.htm.

_______. "The Framework Hypothesis." *Biblical Chronology* 3:6 (June 1991). Also available at http://www.biblicalhorizons.com/biblical-chronology/3_06.

_______, "Waltke on Genesis One." *Biblical Chronology* 10:1 (January 1998). Also available at http://reformed-theology.org/ice/newslet/bc/bc.98.01.htm.

Kay, Marc. "On literary theorists' approach to Genesis 1: Part 1." *Journal of Creation* 21:2 (2007) 71–76. Also available at http://creation.com/images/pdfs/tj/j21_2/j21_2_71-76.pdf.

_______. "On literary theorists' approach to Genesis 1: Part 2." *Journal of Creation* 21:3 (2007) 93–101. Also available at http://creation.com/images/pdfs/tj/j21_3/j21_3_93-101.pdf.

Kelly, Douglas F. *Creation and Change: Genesis 1.1–2.4 in the Light of Changing Scientific Paradigms*. Great Britain: Christian Focus Publications, 1997.

Kruger, Michael J. "An Understanding of Genesis 2:5." *CEN Technical Journal* 11:1 (1997) 106–110. Also available at http://creation.com/images/pdfs/tj/j11_1/j11_1_106-110.pdf.

Kulikovsky, Andrew S. *A Critique of the Literary Framework View of the Days of Creation*. Available at http://hermeneutics.kulikovskyonline.net/hermeneutics/Framework.pdf.

_______. "God's Rest in Hebrews 4:1–11." *Journal of Creation* 13:2 (1999) 61–62. Also available at http://creation.com/gods-rest-in-hebrews-4111.

MacArthur, John. *Genesis 1: Fact or Framework?* Available at http://www.gty.org/Resources/Articles/2422.

McCabe, R. "A Critique of the Framework Interpretation of the Creation Account (Part 1 of 2)." *Detroit Baptist Seminary Journal* 10 (2005) 19–67. Also available at http://www.dbts.edu/journals/2005/McCabe.pdf.

_______. "A Critique of the Framework Interpretation of the Creation Account (Part 2 of 2)." *Detroit Baptist Seminary Journal* 11 (2006) 63–133. Also available at http://www.dbts.edu/journals/2006/McCabe.pdf.

_______. "A Critique of the Framework Interpretation of the Creation Week." In *Coming to Grips with Genesis: Biblical Authority and the Age of the Earth,* ed. Terry Mortenson & Thane H. Ury, 211–250. Green Forest, AR: Master Books, 2008.

Pipa, Joseph A., Jr. "From Chaos to Cosmos: A Critique of the Non-Literal Interpretations of Genesis 1:1–2:3." In *Did God Create in Six Days?* ed. Joseph A. Pipa & David W. Hall, 153–198. Greenville, SC: Southern Presbyterian Press, 1999.

______. *From Chaos to Cosmos: A Critique of the Framework Hypothesis.* Available at http://www.westminsterreformedchurch.org/ScienceMTS/Science.Pipa.Framework.Critique.htm.

Sarfati, Jonathan. "The Numbering Pattern of Genesis: Does It Mean the Days are Non-Literal?" *Journal of Creation* 17:2 (August 2003) 60–61. Also available at http://creation.com/the-numbering-pattern-of-genesis.

Stambaugh, James. "The Days of Creation: A Semantic Approach." *CEN Technical Journal* 5:1 (1991) 70–78. Also available at http://www.creationontheweb.com/content/view/4100.

Steinmann, Andrew. "'*ehad* as an ordinal number and the meaning of Genesis 1:5." *Journal of the Evangelical Theological Society* 45:4 (2002) 577–584.

Vander Hart, Mark. *Bob Godfrey on the Days of Creation*. Available at http://www.banneroftruth.org/pages/articles/article_detail.php?700.

VanDyken, J. C. "The Framework Hypothesis." *The Trumpet* 12:1 (January 2000) 7–9; 12:2 (February 2000) 6–9; 12:3 (March 2000) 6–9; 12:4 (April 2000) 5–8; 12:5 (May 2000) 8–12; 12:6 (June 2000) 8–11.

Vincent, Richard J. *In Defense of God's Creation: A Personal Position Paper*. Available at http://www.theocentric.com/originalarticles/creation.html.

Walker, Frank. "A Critique of the Framework Hypothesis." *Chalcedon Report* 398 (September 1998) 30–34.

_______. "Genesis 1 Versus the Framework Hypothesis." *Reformed Herald* 57:6 (February 2001). Also available at http://spindleworks.com/library/walker/framework01.htm.

Weeks, Noel. "The Hermeneutical Problem of Genesis 1–11." *Themelios* 4 (September 1978) 12–19. Also available at http://www.biblicalstudies.org.uk/pdf/genesis_weeks.pdf.

Witteveen, Jim. *God's Pattern for Creation, by W. Robert Godfrey*. Available at http://www.jimwitt.ca/?postid=329.

Young, Edward J. "The Days of Genesis." *Westminster Theological Journal* 25:1 (1962) 1–34. Also available at http://faculty.gordon.edu/hu/bi/Ted_Hildebrandt/OTeSources/01-Genesis/Text/Articles-Books/Young_Days1a-WTJ.htm.

_______. "The Days of Genesis" (second article). *Westminster Theological Journal* 25:2 (1963) 143–171. Also available at http://faculty.gordon.edu/hu/bi/Ted_Hildebrandt/OTeSources/01-Genesis/Text/Articles-Books/Young_Days2-WTJ.pdf.

Zylstra, Mark. *Re-visiting the days of creation. . . again!* Available at http://spindleworks.com/library/zylstra/framework.htm.

Other studies:

"Is the Seventh Day an Eternal Day?" *Creation* 21:3 (1999) 44–45. Also available at http://creation.com/is-the-seventh-day-an-eternal-day.

The Dort Study Bible. Vol. 1: Genesis - Exodus. Neerlandia, AB: Inheritance, 2003.

Batten, Don, and Jonathan Sarfati. *15 Reasons to Take Genesis as History*. Brisbane: Creation Ministries International, 2006.

Calvin, John. *Commentaries on The First Book of Moses Called Genesis*. Vol. 1. Grand Rapids, MI: Baker Books, 2009. Also available at http://www.ccel.org/ccel/calvin/calcom01.html.

Chaffey, Tim. "An Examination of Augustine's Commentaries on Genesis One and Their Implications on a Modern Theological Controversy." *Answers Research Journal* 4 (2011) 89-101. Also available at http://www.answersingenesis.org/articles/arj/v4/n1/examining-augustine-genesis-commentaries.

Einwechter, William. "The Meaning of 'Day' in Genesis 1–2." *Chalcedon Report* 398 (September 1998) 11–14. Also available at http://www.immanuelfrc.org/articles/15.

Faulkner, Danny. *Universe By Design: An Explanation of Cosmology and Creation*. Green Forest, AR: Master Books, 2004.

Grigg, Russel. "How Long Were the Days of Creation?" *Creation* 19:1 (December 1996) 23–25. Also available at http://creation.com/how-long-were-the-days-of-genesis-1.

Grudem, Wayne. *Systematic Theology: An Introduction to Biblical Doctrine*. Grand Rapids, MI: Zondervan, 1994, 300–304.

Hall, David. *Holding Fast to Creation*. Oak Ridge, TN: The Covenant Foundation, 2001.

Henry, Carl F. H. *God, Revelation and Authority*. Vol. 6: *God Who Stands and Stays, Part* 2. Wheaton, IL: Crossway Books, 1999.

Henry, Matthew. *Commentary on the Whole Bible*. Vol. 1: *Genesis to Deuteronomy*. Peabody, MA: Hendrickson, 1991.

Joüon, Paul. *Grammaire de l'hébreu biblique*. Rome: Institut Biblique Pontifical, 1923.

Keil, C. F., and F. Delitzsch. *Commentary on the Old Testament in Ten Volumes*. Vol. 1: *The Pentateuch*. Grand Rapids, MI: Eerdmans, 1986.

Lavallee, Louis. "Augustine on the Creation Days." *Journal of the Evangelical Theological Society* 32:4 (December 1989) 457–464. Also available at http://www.etsjets.org/files/JETS-PDFs/32/32-4/32-4-pp457-464_JETS.pdf.

Ludwig, Mark. "The War Against Genesis 1." *Chalcedon Report* 398 (September 1998) 14–18.

McCabe, Robert V. "A Defense of Literal Days in the Creation Week." *Detroit Baptist Seminary Journal* 5 (Fall 2000) 97–123. Also available at http://www.dbts.edu/journals/2000/McCabe.pdf.

McIlhenny, Charles A. "Literal, Six-Day Creation and the Local Church." *Chalcedon Report* 398 (September 1998) 34–36.

Rushdoony, R. J. "The Importance of Six-Day Creation." *Chalcedon Report* 398 (September 1998) 2.

Sarfati, Jonathan. *Refuting Compromise: A Biblical and Scientific Refutation of "Progressive Creationism" (Billions of Years), As Popularized by Astronomer Hugh Ross*. Green Forest, AR: Master Books, 2004.

Shaw, Benjamin. "The Literal Day Interpretation." In *Did God Create in Six Days?* ed. Joseph A. Pipa & David W. Hall, 199–220. Greenville, SC: Southern Presbyterian Press, 1999.

Snapp, Byron. "Creating a Controversy." *Chalcedon Report* 398 (September 1998) 19–21.

Taylor, Paul F. *The Six Days of Genesis*. Green Forest, AR: Master Books, 2007.

Van Dam, C. "Creation." *Clarion* 37:24 (Nov. 25, 1988) 486-487; 37:25 (Year End 1988) 516–517; 38:1 (Jan. 3, 1989) 4–5; 38:3 (Feb. 3, 1989) 54–55; 38:4 (Feb. 17, 1989) 74–75; 38:5 (Mar. 3, 1989) 9–95; 38:7 (March 31, 1989) 146–147. Also available at http://www.spindleworks.com/library/vandam/creation.htm#INTRODUCTION.

Young, E. J. "Au commencement Dieu." *La Revue Réformée* 150:2 (June 1987).

______. *In The Beginning: Genesis Chapters 1 to 3 and the Authority of Scripture*. Edinburg: The Banner of Truth Trust, 1976.

______. "The Relation of the First Verse of Genesis One to Verses Two and Three." *Westminster Theological Journal* 21:2 (1959) 133–147.

Positions taken by Seminaries or Churches:

Westminster Theological Seminary and the Days of Creation: A Brief Statement. Available at http://www.wts.edu/about/beliefs/statements/creation.html.

What the Faculty of Mid-America Reformed Seminary Teaches Regarding the Days of Creation. Available at http://www.midamerica.edu/about/docstandards.htm.

Reformed Church in the United States (RCUS):

The Days of Creation: The Report of the Special Committee to Articulate the Doctrine of Creation. Reformed Church in the United States. Adopted by the 253rd Synod of the RCUS. May 17–20, 1999. Available at http://www.rcus.org.

Orthodox Christian Reformed Churches (OCRC):

Orthodox Christian Reformed Church Position Paper on Creation. Available at http://cambridgeocrc.org/Documents/federation/PositionPapers/Creation.htm.

United Reformed Churches (URC):

Minutes of the Fourth Synod of the United Reformed Churches in North America. Escondido, 2001, 20–23, 162–163, 174–175. Available at https://www.urcna.org/sysfiles/site_uploads/pubs/pub3419_1.pdf.

Van Dyk, John. "URC Synod reiterates commitment to confessions on creation." *Christian Renewal* 19:18 (June 2001) 8.

Van Dyken, D. "A Brief Report on the OCRC Synod 2001." *The Trumpet* 13:10 (November 2001) 11.

Presbyterian Church in America (PCA):

"A Declaration. By Westminster Presbytery, PCA." *Chalcedon Report* 398 (September 1998) 21–22.

Report of the Creation Study Committee (Presbyterian Church in America). Available at http://www.pcahistory.org/creation/report.html.

Orthodox Presbyterian Church (OPC):

The Report of the OPC Committee to study the Framework Hypothesis. Presented to the Presbytery of Southern California (OPC) at its Meeting on October 15–16, 1999. Available at http://www.asa3.org/gray/framework/frameworkOPC-SC.html.

"An Assembly Seeking the Lord." *New Horizons* 22:8 (August–September 2001) 8–9. Also available atttp://www.opc.org/nh.html?article_id=95.

Olinger, Danny. "The Seventy-First General Assembly." *New Horizons* 25:8 (August–September 2004) 6–8. Also available at http://www.opc.org/nh.html?article_id=121.

INDEX OF AUTHORS

Aalders, G. C., note 3.
Augustine, 46, 159, 243–244; notes 62, 63.
Batten, Don, 236, 237, 243; notes 185, 188, 269.
Beall, Todd S., 177, 237; note 272.
Bergman, Jerry, notes 269, 270.
Berkhof, Louis, 108; note 179.
Berthoud, Jean-Marc, 90, 237, 238; note 139.
Blocher, Henri, 13, 50, 71, 73, 89, 90, 143, 173, 183, 184, 233, 238; notes 2, 9, 25, 70, 110, 136–138, 141, 170, 219, 260, 261, 283.
Butler, M., 238; note 27.
Byl, John, 176, 237; notes 37, 236, 259, 267, 269, 280, 283.
Calvin, John, 44, 55, 158–161, 192, 243; notes 59, 85, 230, 235.
Chaffey, Timothy R., 237, 243; notes 63, 72, 111, 240, 245, 248, 252, 264, 290.
Clark, R. Scott, notes 200, 211.
Cosner, Lita, 237; note 283.
DeBoer, Louis F., 238; note 247.
Deffinbaugh, Bob, 233; notes 110, 183.
du Toit, François, note 197.
Duncan III, J. Ligon, 32, 234; note 246.
Falk, Darrel, 183; note 285.
Faulkner, Danny, 154–157, 243; notes 96, 115, 227, 228, 269.
Fredricks, C. J., 236; notes 2, 71.
Futato, Mark D., 29, 50, 66, 73, 81, 82, 84, 109, 143, 144, 233;

notes 2, 31, 33, 34, 71, 75, 99, 103, 109, 110, 113, 120, 121, 180, 182, 184, 218, 221.
Gentry, Kenneth L., 27, 238; notes 3, 27, 29, 30, 140, 186.
Godfrey, W. Robert, 15, 23, 31, 37–40, 45–48, 52, 83–87, 96–101, 107, 109, 120, 123, 138, 144, 160, 166, 171, 176, 234, 237, 241, 242; notes 2, 14, 22, 24, 31, 37–39, 49–51, 54, 60, 64–68, 71, 76, 104, 114, 124–131, 149–157, 160–167, 169, 171, 177, 178, 181, 191, 192, 196, 222, 231–236, 242, 253, 259, 267, 268.
Godfrey, Stephen J., 234; notes 117, 203, 212–215, 223–226.
Grigg, Russel, 243; note 257.
Grudem, Wayne, 96, 243; notes 111, 148.
Gunkel, Hermann, 111.
Hall, David W., 32, 234, 243; notes 3, 105, 246.
Hamilton, Victor P., 235; notes 2, 71.
Hanko, Herman, 239; note 250.
Hartnett, John, notes 35, 42, 269.
Hasel, Gerhard F., 239; notes 3, 20, 186.
Henry, Carl F. H., 244; note 57.
Henry, Matthew, 244; note 85.
Horton, Michael Scott, notes 200, 211.
Hughes, R. Kent, 235; notes 2, 71.
Humphreys, Russell, 155; notes 35, 42, 269.
Irons, Lee, 12–15, 32, 41, 72, 74, 78, 82, 84, 104–107, 164, 234, 235; notes 2, 7, 12, 13, 26, 31, 41, 45, 46, 71, 74, 92, 100, 107, 110, 112, 116–118, 122, 168, 174, 175, 238, 246.
Jaeger, Lydia, 183, 235; note 286.
Jordan, James B., 88, 134, 167, 239; notes 3, 30, 72, 111, 113, 132, 180, 199, 202, 240, 244, 245, 259.
Joüon, Paul, 244; notes 61, 83.
Kay, Marc, 13, 91–93, 239; notes 8, 142–144.
Keil, C. F., 244; note 88.
Keller, Tim, 182, 183, 235, 237; notes 141, 282, 283.
Kelly, Douglas F., 91, 240; notes 3, 30, 72, 140, 159, 188.
Kline, Meredith G., 12–15, 23, 32, 33, 36, 37, 41, 49–54, 56, 57, 59–62, 64, 66, 72, 74, 78, 82, 84, 104–107, 133, 134,

136–139, 141–143, 145, 158, 164, 165, 167, 170, 172, 174–176, 180, 184, 191, 192, 234, 235, 239; notes 2, 3, 7, 10–13, 31, 32, 41, 45, 46, 48, 56, 69, 71–74, 77, 80, 81, 89–92, 100, 107, 110–113, 116–118, 122, 168, 174, 175, 217, 238, 240, 241, 245, 246, 259, 262, 263, 265, 283.
Kruger, Michael J., 53, 54, 61, 240; notes 3, 72, 78, 82, 87, 94.
Kulikovsky, Andrew S., 138, 238, 240; notes 3, 24, 30, 111, 133, 159, 210, 240, 255, 278.
Lagrange, M. J., note 2.
Lavallee, Louis, 244; notes 62, 63.
Longman III, Tremper, 178, 179, 181; notes 274, 275.
MacArthur, John, 91, 178, 240; notes 141, 273.
McCabe, Robert V., 26, 82, 94, 128, 240, 244; notes 2, 3, 20, 24, 27, 28, 30, 61, 71, 72, 111, 123, 145, 146, 186, 189, 198, 240, 243, 245.
Nevin, Norman C., note 288.
Noordtzij, Arie, 12, 13, 72, 164; note 110.
Payne, D. F., note 2.
Pipa, Joseph A., Jr., 61, 158, 241; notes 3, 19, 24, 30, 72, 74, 86, 93, 98, 102, 103, 111, 113, 147, 159, 189, 190, 193, 229, 239, 245.
Ramm, Bernard, 235; note 2.
Ridderbos, N. H., 13, 72, 79, 84, 142, 164, 179, 235; notes 2, 95, 106, 109, 110, 119, 216.
Riddlebarger, Kim, notes 200, 211.
Ross, Hugh, 234, 244; notes 20, 288.
Ross, Mark, 39, 67, 73, 104, 107, 236; notes 2, 25, 31, 52, 71, 74, 102, 108, 112, 172, 176.
Sarfati, Jonathan, 237, 241, 243, 244; notes 3, 20, 23, 24, 30, 61, 72, 98, 111, 180, 185, 188, 256, 269, 288.
Shaw, Benjamin, 245; notes 24, 30, 72.
Smith, Christopher R., 136–139, 141, 142, 145, 149–151, 153, 154, 158, 179, 191, 234; notes 2, 117, 203–209, 212–215, 223–226.
Stambaugh, James, 241; notes 20, 186, 255.
Stein, Ben, note 270.
Steinmann, Andrew, 241; note 23.

Thompson, J. A., 181; notes 2, 281.
Throntveit, Mark A., 236; note 2.
Van Dam, C., 245; note 288.
Van Dyk, John, 246; note 279.
Van Dyken, D., 246.
Van Till, Howard H., 179, 180, 236; notes 2, 277, 278.
VanDyken, J. C., 241; notes 3, 6, 12, 251, 254, 259, 266.
Vincent, Richard J., 241; notes 111, 195.
von Herder, Johann Gottfried, 13; note 110.
Walker, Frank, 64, 242; notes 3, 72, 97, 184, 193, 240, 241, 254.
Walker, Tas, note 16.
Wallace, Peter J., 117, 118; note 187.
Waltke, Bruce K., 179, 236, 239; notes 2, 31, 71, 180, 276.
Ward, Rowland S., 21, 23, 236; notes 2, 17, 21, 110, 180.
Weeks, Noel, 143, 147, 184, 242; notes 3, 190, 194, 220, 289.
Wenham, Gordon J., 236; notes 2, 71.
Wise, Kurt, notes 115, 269.
Witteveen, Jim, 47, 100, 242; notes 66, 166, 167, 236.
Young, Edward J., 41, 43, 88, 89, 164, 242, 245; notes 3, 30, 36, 40, 55, 58, 79, 111, 134, 135, 139, 158, 159, 185, 193.
Youngblood, Ronald F., 236; notes 2, 71.
Zylstra, Mark, 242; notes 3, 24, 30, 72, 258.

Churches and organisations:

BioLogos, 182, 183, 235; notes 276, 282–285.
Réseau des scientifiques évangéliques, 183; note 287.
The Days of Creation (RCUS), 246; notes 4, 5, 72.
The Canadian Reformed Churches, note 4.
The Orthodox Christian Reformed Church Position Paper on Creation, 246; notes 4, 44.
The Report of the Creation Study Committee (PCA), 169, 246; notes 4, 249.
The Report of the OPC Committee to study the Framework Hypothesis, 104, 106, 233, 247; notes 4, 25, 31, 32, 47, 71, 110, 173, 201, 237.

CPSIA information can be obtained at www.ICGtesting.com
Printed in the USA
LVOW11s2157200214

374616LV00001B/88/P